LATE BLOOMERS AND EARLY BLOOMERS:

The Sports Science Behind It

by CALLUM MAN

New Degree Press

Copyright © 2020 Callum Man
All rights reserved.

ISBN   978-1-64137-372-2 *Paperback*
            978-1-64137-283-1 *Kindle Ebook*
            978-1-64137-284-8 *Digital Ebook*

Dedicated to Justin Cowen, my close friend who passed away from osteosarcoma at the age of thirteen. Each and every day, he inspires me to reach for the stars. Carrying on my life without him is difficult, but it warms my heart to know how many people still care about him. He is a true inspiration to me and will always be my best friend.

CONTENTS

PART I — **19**

CHAPTER 1: PROBLEMS WITH EARLY BLOOMING — 21
CHAPTER 2: THE PUSH TO BLOOM EARLY — 29
CHAPTER 3: THE PRIZED AJAX ACADEMY — 41

PART II — **49**

CHAPTER 4: PREVENTING BURNOUT — 51
CHAPTER 5: PROFESSIONALISM AND MATURITY — 63
CHAPTER 6: PSYCHOLOGICAL HEALTH — 77
CHAPTER 7: PHYSICAL MATURITY AND INJURIES — 85
CHAPTER 8: BALANCE — 95
CHAPTER 9: FITNESS AND NUTRITION — 105

PART III — **111**

CHAPTER 10: GOAL SETTING — 113
CHAPTER 11: MAXIMIZING DEVELOPMENT — 119
CHAPTER 12: BUILDING A SUPPORT SYSTEM — 129
CHAPTER 13: NUTRITION — 137
CHAPTER 14: UNDERSTANDING LIMITS — 143
CHAPTER 15: RECOVERY — 147

USING THIS BOOK

This book is divided into three main parts that are here to help you learn more about late-blooming and how it applies to your own life. Some chapters may not apply to you, so I have created a guide below for you to find chapters that interest you. Feel free to ignore this section or skip through however you please.

WHAT DO YOU WANT FROM THIS BOOK?
This book is a guide to teach you about early and late-blooming, the effects each has on athletes, and how to apply some of these techniques to your own lives. Depending on what you want out of this book, it may be helpful to skip around and only read certain chapters. Think about where you are as a person. Are you an aspiring athlete, an athlete looking to extend your career, a parent looking to help their kids with sporting decisions, a coach looking to help their athletes? Think about where you stand, and it should help you decide which sections you may or may not want to read.

Another helpful strategy would be to ask yourself why you bought this book. Did you purchase it to learn more about the topic in general? Do you have a reason to become a late bloomer, or are you perhaps an early bloomer looking to capitalize on your competitive advantages? Do you want to seek advice for your child? Do you want advice for coaching? These questions can help decide what you want to get out of this book.

LOOK BEYOND THE NORMAL STRUCTURE

This book, as I said before, is divided into three parts. Each part has its own significance. The first discusses the fallacy of late-blooming, the second discusses principles of late-blooming, and the third discusses how you yourself can become a late bloomer. However, this structure does not really need to concern you. You can use this structure to find the chapters you want to read, but this book does not need to be read in chronological order. Feel free to skip around and read however feels most natural to you.

SKIP THE BORING

This book talks about a lot, and some of the information contained in it might bore you to death. But you have the liberty to skip to whatever sections interest you. If something bores you, skip it — simple as that.

A SHORT GUIDE

If you are looking for some guidance on which sections might apply to you, use the following guide below. But as I have said above, in no way are you obligated to follow this structure.

- For Parents
    - Introduction
    - Chapter 2
    - Chapter 4
    - Chapter 11
    - Chapter 12

- For Coaches
    - Chapter 2
    - Chapter 3
    - Chapter 10
    - Chapter 12
    - Chapter 15

- For Aspiring Athletes*
    - Chapter 4
    - Chapter 6
    - Chapter 8
    - Chapter 10
    - Chapter 11
    - Chapter 12
    - Chapter 13

*If you belong to this category, however, I highly recommend reading the majority of the book.

PREFACE

The sport I know and love has different names around the world. In my country of birth, we refer to the sport as soccer, while the rest of the world refers to it as football. Since I have family in England, I grew up using both terms. In this book, I will use the term football to refer to the sport many call soccer.

My aim in this book is to explore the sports science behind late and early bloomers in football; I want to examine the advantages and disadvantages of each of them respectively. My goal is to give you an insight into the sport of soccer, specifically as it relates to early and late bloomers.

The book is heavily influenced by my opinions, particularly when I analyze the successes and failures of certain athletes. As an avid football fan, remaining objective is virtually impossible. Humans naturally carry various biases, implicit and explicit, but the soul of the book will be built around sports science. Together, we will analyze the physical, emotional, and mental benefits of being a late bloomer.

Football is my hobby and not my profession. I am no expert in sports science. Therefore, I interviewed many experts in their field while writing this book to gain insight into this topic. I also researched countless journals, books, and sites to find accurate information.

By no means is this a perfect product. However, some of the information may be controversial. Sports science itself has always existed in a controversial space. Like the sport of football, many concepts in sports science have long been heavily debated. Regardless, you can still find value in the research and opinions I discuss.

In my study of both late and early bloomers, I began to notice trends that may be highly controversial. My research began to stand in favor of late bloomers, as they enjoyed more benefits in the long term. My book explores these benefits, how they can be applied to any athlete, and how those in their support systems can also help. I divided the book into three distinct parts to make it easier to navigate.

The first part is an introduction to late-blooming in sports. It explores the current state of youth sports and dives into fallacies of early and late-blooming.

The second part is geared toward teaching you about different aspects of blooming late. Each aspect has stories from both early and late bloomers to help paint the picture. We dive into the science behind many of these aspects and begin to see the benefits of late-blooming.

The third and final part will teach you how to apply techniques in your own life, becoming a late bloomer yourself. Each section teaches you about a different aspect of becoming a successful athlete and is intended to help you apply these techniques to your own life.

INTRODUCTION

Early bloomers.

We can all think of one.

I know I saw many from the ages of five to nine. At that time, I began playing lots of different sports: basketball, football, and even baseball. I eventually quit most of these sports because they simply didn't interest me. In each of them, however, I noticed a few kids who were leagues ahead of the rest of us—so much faster, stronger, and more athletic.

When I was about six years old, I can remember two of my football teammates who were leagues ahead of everyone else. I would pass the ball to one of them and, within a few seconds, the ball would hit the back of the opposition's net. Both were incredible, dribbling past the other clueless children with such ease. Everything came naturally to them; the ball stuck to their feet. Whenever they approached the goal—which happened quite frequently—they would hammer the ball toward the net harder and faster than anyone else could. The goalkeepers were always left helpless. It felt criminally unfair, like a game of adults against kids. Football came so naturally to them, and they dominated the sport so easily.

Starting in first grade, both began playing on more competitive teams. They would practice multiple times per week with professional coaches, playing almost nonstop. After a few years, however, the rest of us caught up with them; some even surpassed them in terms of ability. They both had an inborn talent for the sport, but they were never mentally prepared to work on the other attributes of the game. At first, they were faster and stronger than their opponents, but once everyone else caught up, the areas in which they lacked were exposed. I was able to surpass them, and they later quit to focus on other activities. In my opinion, the dream to become an early bloomer has always been outrageous.

**

Pushing to become an early bloomer is practically putting yourself at a disadvantage. This is evident not only from my own youth south career but from all levels of the sport.

**

Those kids peaked earlier than the rest of us and dominated football at a young age, but what about the ones who bloom later? What about those who dominate their sport later in their career?

Consider the example of Miroslav Klose, among the most famous German footballers of his generation. His career began quite anonymously in the fourth division of German football—at the time, the lowest division of professional football in Germany. Klose only began to move up in the ranks and gain recognition later in his career.

Klose—despite not receiving another contract from his team, FC 08 Homburg—still managed to make a name for himself.[1] He eventually established himself as the star forward for the German national football team, where he came to hold the record for most goals in FIFA World Cup History for men's teams. Success stories like Klose's make me wonder about the emphasis so many parents and young athletes place on peaking early and dominating youth sports.

From a technical standpoint, Klose was never the best footballer. His technique and abilities were limited. His pathway to the top, however, was largely influenced by the extra time he took getting there. We hear nowadays of young people playing at the highest level at sixteen or seventeen, but Klose slowly rose to that point.

As he rose through the ranks, Klose observed others around him and was able to hone his own skills through observation. By being an observer and a late bloomer, Klose learned more about the game and more about professionalism.

When Klose eventually got his break, all his time observing and learning from senior players around him paid off. His breadth of knowledge about football, along with his intelligent movement and play style, helped turn him into one of the most famous finishers in World Cup history. His trainability helped him learn and grow into a legendary player.[2]

---

[1] Philcox, Matt. 2017 "Rags to Riches: 9 of Football's Late Bloomers." 90min.Com.

[2] Schulder, Michael. 2017 "The Late-Bloomer Advantage in Sports." Huff-Post.

**

Peaking early is perceived as essential for young athletes hoping to play professionally, and parents push their children for this exact reason. In countries where youth sports are divided into age groups, like Canada, parents try to optimize their child's chances of domination within that group by planning their birth date. If a certain age group required children born between September 2014 and August 2015, for example, parents may aim for a September baby to give them an advantage in youth sports leagues. Dominating in youth sports, however, can cause a multitude of problems that hold athletes back later in their careers.

For most early bloomers, dominating youth sports leads to an inflated ego. They begin to think they are too good and don't need to work as hard as their peers. This perception can severely limit them, since other athletes may begin catching up to them. For early bloomers, finding easy success at a young age may discourage them when they face challenges or aren't dominating later. Often, this can lead to them quitting. The state of youth sports as an entity already makes it difficult for early bloomers to find long-term success in their careers.[3]

Youth sports have become incredibly competitive in the modern day. Parents are competing to get their children onto the best teams and the elite football academies in their area, hoping their children will become successful athletes. From incredibly young ages, kids are thrown into footballing

---

3   Ezez. 2019 "Peaking Too Soon." *NLP Academy*.

academies with rigorous routines and long hours; many also travel long distances to play games or attend practices. The high intensity of these programs and games hurts athletes in the long run; many of these children pick up all kinds of injuries—concussions, ACL injuries, knee injuries—due to the rigor and intensity of the program.

These issues can even be glimpsed on the professional level. Footballer Marco Van Basten, who bloomed early, struggled with injury problems that eventually caused him to retire prematurely. Van Basten was among the best forwards of his generation but injuries shortened his career and his time at the top. Later on, we will explore why so many early bloomers face struggles like these, and we will begin to understand the negatives of early blooming.

**

Not only does dominating youth sports come with drawbacks but peaking later in your career can have serious benefits. Late bloomers often enjoy incredibly long and successful careers. This comes down to many factors like mentality but also how they care for their bodies.

Many late bloomers come to understand the game very well by observing and learning from those around them. Their additional time spent on their journey to the top allows them to work on their skills and learn more about the sport. Athletes like Italian footballer Luca Toni exemplify this phenomenon; although it took some time for Toni to reach his potential, he grew into a football star and played until he was thirty-eight years old.

Luca Toni began his career playing in the lower divisions of Italian football. Toni played in the second and third divisions and changed clubs quite frequently. Yet his fortune began to change as he neared his twenty-eighth birthday.

Toni became a menacing forward, seemingly out of nowhere. He quickly lit up the first division of Italian football, scoring twenty goals in his first season there. His incredible performance earned him a move to ACF Fiorentina, where he would continue to dazzle and demonstrate his goal-scoring touch.

He soon moved up to the Italian national team and helped lead the Italians to victory at the 2006 World Cup. He would go on to play for countless top teams like FC Bayern Munich.[4]

Even as he neared the end of his career, Toni still thrived at the top level. He won the title of *capocannoniere—granted to the top scorer in the Italian Serie A—in one of his final professional seasons.*

As a late bloomer, Toni was able to not only reach incredible heights as a footballer but also to play at that level for a long period of time. He played into his late thirties, a rare opportunity for professional footballers. However, the phenomenon of late-blooming is prevalent in all sports—not just football.

Athletes like Tom Brady epitomize the benefits of peaking later. Brady started his NFL career as the 199th pick in the 2000 NFL

---

4   Harmer, Alfie Potts. 2017 "Seven Greatest Late Bloomers in Football History." *HITC.*

Draft. Over the course of his career, however, Brady has gained many accolades; many credit him as being among the best, if not the greatest, NFL player of all time. In Brady's case, as for many other athletes, peaking later brought many benefits.

The widespread belief in early blooming is a fallacy. Many athletes who bloom early struggle with injuries, burnout, psychological issues, and some even fail to make the professional stage. Blooming later brings with it better success and longevity. Fredua "Freddy" Adu—among the most famous failed wonder-kids of his generation—seems to epitomize the fallacy in early blooming. Commonly forgotten success stories like Luca Toni's, however, demonstrate the benefits of blooming late.

PART I

Chapter 1:
PROBLEMS WITH EARLY BLOOMING

January 16th, 2004: the day of the widely-anticipated Major League Soccer SuperDraft. Many rumblings were going around about a young player, Freddy Adu, a fourteen-year-old who had been making a name for himself since he immigrated to the United States. That night, Adu was drafted as the number-one pick, becoming the highest-paid player in the league and the youngest athlete in the history of American sports. That night, Adu's name ran across newspapers worldwide; they began dubbing him the next Pelé. The world began to expect the world from him; they expected him to revolutionize football in America and achieve true greatness—a heavy burden for someone yet to reach puberty.[5]

Fifteen years come and gone, however, Adu was just recently released from the Las Vegas Lights FC, among the worst teams in the United Soccer League—the second division of

---

5   Keidel, Phil. 2017 "Charting Where It All Went Wrong for 'New Pele' Freddy Adu." *Bleacher Report*.

American football. Adu skyrocketed to fame and fortune but his meteoric descent happened just as quickly. Nowadays, Freddy Adu is a forgotten name—another failed wonder-kid.[6]

His story began in Ghana, his birthplace. There, he started playing football and was still playing when he immigrated to the United States at the age of eight. In Maryland, Adu continued his footballing journey, catching the eyes of many spectators and coaches. In a preseason tournament hosted by the then state-champion Potomac Cougars, Adu shocked those in attendance with his ability, control of the ball, and eye for the goal. His dribbling ability and his scoring were at another level; he would wade past defenders with ease. The game seemed too easy for him. Arnold Tarzy, the head coach of the Cougars at the time, said, "What I saw was beyond realistic."[7]

Grabbing others' attention became routine for Adu, as word began to spread about the talent of this eight-year-old. Negative rumors also began to spread; many questioned his legitimacy, believing he had faked his age as other footballers had before him.

Parents demanded to see his birth certificate to validate Adu's age. These comments hurt Adu; one of his teammates, Nicholas Scrivens, said he once saw Adu crying over the comments

---

6   Togher, Liam, et al. 2019 "Freddy Adu: the Ultimate Case of Unfulfilled Potential." *Football Bloody Hell*.
7   Helms, Andrew. 2016 "Throwback Thursday: 14-Year-Old Freddy Adu and the Age Truthers." *Vice*

about his age.[8] Parents would also encourage their kids to purposely hurt Adu, subjecting him to critical, dangerous tackles, but his dogged mentality and strong motivation kept him going when things were tough. Scrivens also said, "Guys would clean him out on purpose, and he would just get back up... He had that spirit where it was relentless. Freddy wanted to beat you at everything."

Adu's relentless work ethic helped him attract attention from scouts worldwide; from all across Europe, they came to watch the young man play, hoping to see the wonder-kid for themselves. Some even offered Adu contracts and to take him to Europe and join prestigious European academies; one of the top clubs in Italy, Inter Milan, offered Adu's family $750,000 in compensation if he enrolled in their academy. His mother, however, decided against allowing her son to move away to Europe, having immigrated to the United States only a few years prior. She wanted him to focus on football within the United States before moving abroad. As he edged closer to age fourteen, Adu continued to wow audiences, leading his local club team to national glory; he was also called up to the United States men's national under-17 soccer team (U17).

Then came his sudden rise to stardom. He impressed the U17 coaches and staff, raising his stock even higher. Freddy quickly became an overnight sensation: he was drafted by D.C. United, signed a million-dollar deal with Nike, and was featured in magazines and newspapers worldwide. He began to break records as the youngest player and goal-scorer

---

8   Helms, Andrew. 2016 "Throwback Thursday: 14-Year-Old Freddy Adu and the Age Truthers." *Vice*

in MLS history. His name on the roster spiked audience numbers for D.C. United to record levels. All seemed bright for Adu.

Then, however, coaches began complaining about him. They claimed Adu struggled to adapt to life as a professional; the amount of media coverage and sponsorship deals he received did not help matters. Trevor Moawad, a sports psychologist who worked with Adu, claimed he was not given the support he needed to help him develop. "If there was a plan to develop Freddy, I had never heard anything about it," Moawad said. But by the end of his first season, he had picked up five goals, three assists, and played in thirty games. Things looked bright for the young star, but as his reputation continued to grow, so did the media attention.[9]

Adu lasted a few more seasons at D.C. United, racking up eleven goals and seventeen assists in his three years at the club. He continued to attract attention from top clubs around the world. Sir Alex Ferguson and Manchester United FC soon called him in for a trial. "He is a talented boy... we will have to assess what we can do next," said Ferguson. Adu was performing well and the hype surrounding him continued to grow.

But his popularity began to hurt him. "I found myself having to make appearances everywhere. For advertisements, for an enormous amount of interviews," Adu explained. "All of this pushed me away from the field, even though I was still so young... people saw me as only a marketing product." The large amount of media attention he received pulled him away

---

9   Ezez. 2019 "Freddy Adu." *MLS*

from the sport and distracted him, even hurt his feelings. One of Adu's close friends explained how the attention hurt him; the negative comments about him had escalated from his time as a youth athlete. All this made it difficult for Adu to focus on football, and in the coming season, his fast and rapid decline would begin.

In Adu's last season at D.C. United, he had a falling out with the manager. He complained about a lack of playing time, which caused the manager to ship him away to Real Salt Lake, a nearby MLS team. Adu spent only half a year there, as his impressive performances in the U20 World Cup earned him a move to S.L. Benfica, his first European football club.

With Adu's move to European football came the downfall of his career. Over the next few years, he would underwhelm at numerous clubs and would find himself being thrown out season after season. He played all across Europe—Portugal, France, Greece, Turkey—but in each country struggled to get game time and lost favor with his manager. After facing rejection all across Europe, Adu took his mother's advice and returned to the States, joining Philadelphia Union. Many thought this transfer would set his career back into motion; fans thought he would find his form again and live up to the potential everyone knew he had.[10]

Back in the United States, he was reunited with his former boss from D.C. United, Peter Nowak. Times began to change for Adu; he picked up some form and even earned himself a

---

10   Gottlieb, Jeremy. 2019. "Freddy Adu Makes 'Decision' to Return to Professional Soccer." *The Washington Post*.

spot in the United States men's national football team.[11] This sudden rise in form would not last, however, as he would fall out with yet another manager and would be sent out to a Brazilian outfit, Bahia. Disaster struck yet again for Adu, and after another failed season, the club released him. Nowadays, Freddy Adu is a forgotten man, a failed wonder-kid. Yet his story is hardly unique; hundreds and hundreds of young athletes like Freddy peak too early and lose their careers along the way.

Adu's situation wasn't entirely his fault, either. The environment where he began wasn't ready for a young American football star. When Adu broke onto the scene, most people around him saw him only as a marketing product rather than a person and a player. He never learned the discipline or the work ethic of a professional player.

Another player who struggled to capitalize on his potential is British footballer Ravel Morrison. Coaches and players gave him a strong and supportive environment for him to grow, but off-the-field distractions and troubles began to absorb his interests. His troubled upbringing, as well as the lack of a strong support system from his family drove Morrison to crime.[12] For prospective athletes, developing a strong support system is pivotal for success.

Additionally, in Morrison's case, he was not motivated to focus on football because of childhood mental trauma.

---

[11] Schoenfeld, Bruce, 2011 "Freddy Adu." *ESPN*

[12] Pilger, Sam. 2017. "The £50 Million Prodigy Better Than Pogba: Can Ravel Morrison Save His Career?". *Bleacher Report*.

Mental health plays a large role in an athlete's success, and without the correct support systems, they will struggle.

Even players like Patrick Kluivert and Wayne Rooney—early bloomers who had successful careers—have struggled to stay at the top level. Wayne Rooney is a Manchester-United legend but struggled with longevity.

Rooney burst onto the scene as a sixteen-year-old boy playing for Everton FC, which caught the attention of Manchester United. Over the next few seasons, he would write his name into the history books of Manchester United; at the age of thirty, however, when most athletes reach their prime, Rooney found himself benched. He struggled for game time even among a weak Manchester-United team. Rooney would be sold off into the MLS, where his career would slowly die down.

Rooney's problem was his work ethic. He began his career with an incredibly high work ethic, putting his heart and soul into every game he played. His position as a striker wore down his legs, however, and he would regularly overwork himself in training. The resultant wear on Rooney's body made it difficult to continue playing for Manchester United. If he had a more balanced lifestyle and was more cautious with his play style, he would have enjoyed a longer, more successful career.

Finding both success and longevity is incredibly difficult for footballers. Many football players only manage one of the two, if either. One footballer may have an incredibly long career but find little success, while another footballer may find success in a short career.

Many struggle to find a balance between the two, but early bloomers can find both longevity and success in their career if they take the correct approaches. We will also discover how late bloomers often find both success and longevity.

Chapter 2:
THE PUSH TO BLOOM EARLY

Zlatan Ibrahimović, one of the greatest players of his generation, grew up in severe poverty. In his autobiography, he outlines the struggles he faced as a kid. Ibrahimović grew up in the ghetto of Malmö, where both of his parents struggled to make ends meet. His parents divorced and life in Malmö was difficult; he had to steal and quite literally fight to survive. Football, however, saved Ibrahimović. His footballing abilities helped him get away from his circumstances; he was offered a chance to play for a local Swedish club and eventually became one of the best players in the world. Ibrahimović didn't have money, but his talent helped him out of his difficult financial situation. If Ibrahimović had grown up in America, however, his situation would have been completely different.

**

The structure of American sports is incredibly unique. In America, any young athlete must pay a local club, team, or organization to play a sport officially. Additionally, they must pay for equipment, which can be incredibly costly depending on the sport. Even football can be outrageously expensive—playing for a basic recreational football program can cost hundreds of dollars. If your child wants to play at a higher level, you'll have to pay even more, potentially thousands of dollars. These high expenses hurt participation in American organized sports. Many low-income families cannot afford to put their kids on their local team; these children, in turn, have far less chance of going professional.

In the last few years, participation in organized sports in America has decreased significantly. The number of six- to twelve-year-olds in America participating in youth sports has fallen nearly fifteen percent in the last three years, according to a 2018 study by the Sports & Fitness Industry Association (SFIA).[13] Americans—especially lower-income Americans—are less likely to have children who participate in sports because of growing expenses. In fact, only thirteen percent of all six- to twelve-year-olds who play football in America belong to families with an income of $25,000 or less.[14] This pay-to play-model limits the majority of young people from becoming better football players. On this issue, Hope Solo, a former goalkeeper for the United States women's national soccer team, said, "My family would not have been able to afford to put me in football if I was a young kid today."[15] The cost of these programs is problematic and

---

[13] Ezez. 2016. "7 Charts that Show the State of Youth Sports in the US and Why it Matters - The Aspen Institute". *The Aspen Institute*.

[14] Thompson, Derek. 2018 "American Meritocracy Is Killing Youth Sports." *The Atlantic*.

[15] Cook, Bob. 2018. "What's Killing Youth Soccer in America Is Also Hurting Most Every Other Sport." *Forbes*.

neglects major crops of talent. In many other countries, like England or the Netherlands, footballing academies invest in their own players. These academies pay for their athletes to attend schools and do not require athletes or their parents to pay to play. This has enabled many lower-income footballers to become professional stars despite their humble beginnings.

Daniel Alves, one of the most decorated footballers of all time, also struggled financially as a young kid. He helped his father with work daily before walking or biking twelve miles to school and back; his father worked multiple jobs, struggling to get by financially. Eventually, Alves was scouted and given a chance to play for a Brazilian club, which offered to house him and provide him with food and training. He slowly worked his way up the ladder and was eventually recruited to play for FC Barcelona and Juventus FC. Alves won many accolades over his long career as an attacking wingback, ending his career with over forty trophies. If he was raised in America, however, he would never have become a professional. American sports are too heavily dependent on the parent to help pay for their child to play. This creates many problems, as the wealthier parents degrade cheaper levels of youth sports.

Americans who can afford to play at the higher levels hurt youth participation in sports as a whole. More affluent parents tend to send their children to high-level, expensive teams. This removes competition in the cheaper leagues, which then causes many kids in cheaper leagues to quit. Children want to play at a high level, and the inability to afford that level can discourage them from playing.

Many affluent parents will also try to better their child with elite and specialized coaching; they also send their children to expensive camps to help them develop to their full potential. This hurts other athletes, as it creates these barriers between the wealthier kids and the poorer kids who cannot afford specialized training. As more money is poured into youth football in America, all that money is funneled into paying expensive coaches and enhancing expensive clubs. This money should, instead, be directed toward less fortunate and less affluent athletes. In the current system, their talent is often neglected for financial reasons.

The underlying problem is the American system of capitalism; this system encourages clubs to build a pay-to-play model. This model has, in turn, lowered the quality of the United States men's national team, which has recently struggled to qualify for international tournaments. The Norwegian approach to youth sports, in contrast, is more egalitarian—offering more athletes the chance to make it professionally.

The Norwegians, overall, are more focused on being egalitarian. Their government-run lottery is used to support and fund youth sports in Norway. Norwegians hardly pay to enroll their children in local teams or academies, which gives all Norwegian children the chance to grow and develop into stars. They value participation over the hyper-competitive and intense models we have in America, and their track record is proven: many footballing icons have thrived from this model.[16] Two of these icons are Ole

---

[16] Thompson, Derek. 2018 "American Meritocracy Is Killing Youth Sports." *The Atlantic*.

Gunnar Solskjær, a legendary Manchester United striker, and Ada Hegerberg, the 2018 winner of the women's Ballon d'Or award. The Norwegians have found much success in their minimal-cost model and their focus on participation over competition.

Norway brought home thirty-nine medals in the 2018 Winter Olympics, the most of any country in the competition. The American pay-to-play model struggled to find as much success as the Norwegian egalitarian model, despite large population differences between the two countries: 327.2 million US Americans to 5.2 million Norwegians.[17]

In America, an emphasis on playing at the highest level leads elite football clubs to require athletes to try out for their teams. Along with this comes a huge emphasis on sports specialization—athletes only focusing on one sport. According to a 2016 study from the American Academy of Pediatrics, sports specialization leads to an "increase in overuse injuries, overtraining and burnout." According to that same study, concussion rates among football players ages seven to seventeen have risen 11.4 percent.[18] Hyper-focusing on one sport hurts the development of an athlete and, ultimately, their career. Other studies have found no inherent difference in success between a specialized football athlete and a non-specialized multi-sport football athlete prior to puberty.

---

17 Britton, Bianca. 2018. "The secret behind Norway's Winter Olympic success". *CNN*.

18 Flanagan, Linda. 2018 "The Downsides of America's Hyper-Competitive Youth-Soccer Industry." *The Atlantic*.

However, the system of privatized football clubs is hurting the development of many players. Private clubs often require an excessive amount of travel for children on their team; on weekends and even weekdays, kids must travel for hours to get to practice or a game. This practice increases specialization in football and makes injuries more likely; it also takes a toll on players socially, as leagues prevent club players from playing for their school team. This can isolate many club players, separating them from friends and hurting their overall morale. Additionally, this emphasis on playing for a private, expensive team creates a hyper-competitive sporting culture among these athletes.

Over the years, increased competition in youth sports has increased the desire among youth athletes to bloom early. The footballing world globally, too, has grown even more competitive; clubs are spending millions of dollars each year to improve training facilities and bring in the best coaches and players. As the sport continues to grow, more emphasis is placed on footballing academies and youth recruitment. Especially following the success of the Ajax Youth Academy and La Masia—academies that have produced some of the best talent in the world—clubs are looking to reinvest in scouting and recruiting for young prodigies.

From 2009–2011, FC Barcelona was the dominant footballing team, winning excessive amounts of trophies; they won La Liga, Copa del Rey, and the elusive UEFA Champions League. Barcelona not only won a historic treble—three trophies in a single season—but did it with eleven crucial players having come from La Masia, the FC Barcelona Academy.[19] This event kickstarted a global movement toward investing in sporting academies; more and more clubs began to invest in their own footballing facilities and coaching staff. More clubs began to focus their attention on scouting and recruiting new talent, hoping to make them into professional players. This attitude, however, is problematic for young, developing athletes.

Nowadays, scouting begins at incredibly young ages, which encourages young athletes to strive for blooming early. With academies scouting kids at the tender age of seven, the stakes have never been higher; kids push themselves, or parents push their children, to bloom early in the hopes of being scouted. This phenomenon is known as over-identification—a common trait among parents. Over-identification is described as a tendency for parents to push for their child to be the best, mainly for the interests of the parents.[20] Over-identification occurs more than you might expect and creates many problems for children later in life.

Pushing to become a professional athlete means specializing in one specific sport. Sports specialization can be incredibly dangerous, especially for younger athletes. A 2018 study by the American Academy of Pediatrics, which studied athletes below age eighteen, compared single-sport and multi-sport athletes. Their results showed highly-specialized athletes were at greater risk of injury compared to athletes compared

---

19   Ezez. 2019 "FC Barcelona - Club Profile 08/09." *Transfermarkt*.
20   Firestone, Lisa. 2013 "The Dangers of Narcissistic Parents." *Psychology Today*.

to non-specialized athletes[21] This generally means young, specialized athletes have an incredibly high risk of injury—especially given high dedication to that sport. By playing other sports or playing less intensely, the risk of injury falls dramatically. The environment of competitive youth sports in America, however, encourages kids to specialize at a young age—becoming increasingly prone to long-term injuries.

Athletes are risking their own health and the longevity of their careers in the hope of being scouted from an early age. Although a rise in scouting and recruiting has contributed to the push to bloom early, the prevalence of social media in the modern day has made the dream of becoming a professional athlete seem more attainable than ever.

We see lots of hype around young athletes in our day and age, hype which pressures them to become one of the greats of the footballing world. Although many do not reach the heights expected of them, those who do make an imprint on us. When kids see young players like Pelé or Messi turning the world alight during their teenage years, it inspires them to push to bloom early like their heroes; when they see young stars flourishing under pressure, they dream about doing so themselves. However, when they see these examples, they see an attainable goal. They push for it, pushing to become the footballing star who writes the headlines, the dominant athlete at youth levels; they overwork themselves in hopes of becoming the next teenage star. The stories we hardly ever see, though, are about wonder-kids who failed

---

21 Bell, David. 2018. "Sport Specialization and Risk of Overuse Injuries: A Systematic Review With Meta-analysis. - PubMed - NCBI". *NCBI*.

because of their early rise to the top. We hardly ever see articles about Freddy Adu; as the news is filled with success stories. Parents have to come to grips with this reality for themselves; they are at the forefront of this push to bloom early and have helped contribute to this toxic, hyper-competitive environment.

Parents try to influence the athletic careers of their children. Some plan their child's birthday to give them an advantage over their peers, called the calendar-based advantage. The calendar based-advantage is the phenomenon of parents wanting their child to be the oldest of their age group, hoping they will then be bigger, stronger, and faster than the younger kids of that group. The benefits of the calendar-based advantage are highly debated; many recent studies have both proven and disproven the theory.

A few studies have been done which have supported benefits of the calendar-based advantage in football; one study performed by Roger Barnsley and Gus Thompson looked at the effects of a calendar-based advantage on athletes playing competitively in their countries. They began by researching athletes who participated in the 1989 U17 World Cup, the 1989 U20 World Cup, and the 1990 World Cup. The study divided the football year into quarters based on cut-off lines for the U17 and U20 World Cups. Then, each athlete was categorized by their quarter and birth and their data was logged into a Chi-square table, to compare the data. In each tournament studied, data distribution heavily favored the first quarter—the oldest age group. For the U17 and U20 World Cups, the percentage of athletes born in the first quarter was marginally higher than for the senior World Cup; U20 had a first-quarter percentage of 44.95, U17 of 46.87, and the World Cup of only 28.41. The age distribution overall was more diverse in the senior group; each quarter had around twenty-five percent of the crop.[22] This statistic suggests the validity of the calendar advantage at the youth level; however, the advantage does not apply to senior levels of play. At the other end of the spectrum, more recent studies have suggested different results.

A series of studies done by Gavin Sandercock, who tested boys and girls between the ages of ten and sixteen, found athletes born in November and October performed better overall in physical examinations. Those born in November and October performed better than their counterparts in strength, stamina, and cardiovascular fitness; this data seems to disprove the calendar-based advantage.[23] According to this study, athletes born later in the year perform better, but parents continue to plan their child's birth date.

Despite how outrageous it may seem, parents strategize about birth dates in hopes of giving their child an advantage. Such an intense push to bloom early can come from the parents as much as, or even more so, than from children themselves. Parents enroll their kids in elite training camps and stress the importance of competing and winning—strategies with drastic downsides for the future of their child.

---

22 Barnsley, Roger H.; Thompson, A.H. & Legault, Philipe. 1992. "Family Planning: Football Style. The Relative Age Effect in Football". *International Review for the Sociology of Sport* 27 (1): 77-87. SAGE Publications. doi:10.1177/101269029202700105.

23 Moss, Tyler. 2015 "How to Conceive an Athlete." *The Cut*.

The push to bloom early stems from a variety of factors but is ultimately toxic for the modern game. As these children begin specializing in sports and enter hyper-competitive leagues, they risk injury in the long run. This emphasis on blooming early is hurting the development of American athletic talents, but even some of the best footballing academies struggle with early bloomers. Despite the successes of the Ajax Academy over the past few decades, even the most established academies seem to struggle with early blooming.

Chapter 3:
THE PRIZED AJAX ACADEMY

Look up the greatest footballer of all time. One of the first names you will see is Johan Cruyff. As a manager and player, Cruyff is among the most influential people in the history of football. Let's take a look at how he gained his many accolades.

Cruyff began his footballing career playing in the local parks. At age ten, he signed his first contract with the prestigious Ajax Academy; there, Cruyff's career began to take flight. After a few years, he began to impress on the senior team, racking up 190 goals in just 240 games. Cruyff later went to play for prestigious clubs like FC Barcelona, where he would further establish his legacy as a footballing icon.

On the pitch, Cruyff was known for his intelligence, creating new maneuvers that are still used today, like the Cruyff turn. His playing style influenced an entire generation of footballers. Cruyff later returned to football as a manager, where his intelligence would truly begin to show.

Cruyff returned to Ajax Academy and would change the club for the better. He developed a possessive footballing style called Tiki Taka, which is heavily reliant on possession and movement. Cruyff instilled a playing philosophy that has stuck at Ajax, helping to turn the academy into a talent factory.

AFC Ajax has played host to many legendary players over the years, like Johan Cruyff, Frank Rijkaard, and Dennis Bergkamp. When these superstars joined the club, however, they were not household names; they were young prodigies hoping to make it professionally. Over the years, Ajax has earned a reputation as a wonderful academy and prides itself on its ability to develop players into global superstars. Ajax Academy has become a sort of talent factory, producing new young stars who are then snatched up by other top clubs.[24] The youth system at Ajax, like many youth systems in Europe, contrasts starkly with youth sports in America. European academies like Ajax should set the precedent for how youth sports should be run.

Ajax has further perfected its model over the years and developed its own philosophy for scouting players, looking at unique aspects in a young athlete. Ajax scouts venture around Amsterdam and nearby cities in Holland to identify potential stars. Unlike many scouting systems worldwide, however, Ajax scouts look less for physical attributes and more for technical aspects.

Ronald de Jong, a scout for Ajax, said, "I am never looking for a result—for example, which boy is scoring the most goals or

---

24 Coppack, Sean & Eoghan Macguire. 2019. "Inside Ajax's $500 Million Football Factory." *CNN*.

even who is running the fastest. That may be because of their size and stage of development. I want to notice how a boy runs. Is he on his forefeet, running lightly? Does he have creativity with the ball? Does he seem that he is really loving the game? I think these things are good at predicting how he'll be when he is older."[25] Ajax scouts focus on passing, movement, and dribbling skills, rather than the physical development of an athlete. These scouts understand athletes develop at different stages and will mature later on in life. They prize the technically-skilled, intelligent player over the strong, athletic one.[26] Not all scouts see it the same way, however.

In England, scouts are notorious for rejecting players for being too small or too weak. Over the past few years, this has been problematic for the English national team and English football overall. Many players have been rejected for being too small. Taller, stronger players are chosen over them, but these players often lack key attributes of the game—a fact which is exposed further down the line. Few of them make it to the professional scene and their rejected counterparts do not even get a chance.

In fact, my father encountered this exact phenomenon growing up in England. My father never looked to play professionally but once ended up playing against a young prodigy on his school's football team. At the time, one of the opposition's players—a big, tall defender—played for the youth

---

25 Sokolove, Michael. 2010 "How a Soccer Star Is Made." *The New York Times*.
26 Ezez. 2017. "A.F.C. Ajax's Youth Development Philosophy with Arnold Mühren - generation adidas international". *generation adidas international*

national team and was surrounded by hype. My father played that game as a striker, an unfamiliar position for him, but managed to score a hat-trick despite being marked by the national team player. Spectators were shocked to see this young English prodigy struggle against a makeshift striker.

My father kept tabs on the player; he never ended up playing for the senior team, only the third tier of English football. Ultimately, he had no special attributes; he was merely big and tall at the time. This situation is hardly unique, however, but is exemplified by a current English national team that lacks small, technical players.

In the semifinal game of the 2018 FIFA World Cup against Croatia, the English team struggled to hold possession and create goal-scoring chances. This demonstrates the value in scouting the Ajax way; they seem to have a more reliable method of finding the next star.

After being selected by scouts, children are thrown into a professional environment. They begin training daily with other scouted athletes. The program is highly intensive; as the years go on, more players are told not to return, while newer prospects are brought in to replace them. Scouted athletes remain in school but Ajax buses transport them from school to Ajax training facilities after the day has ended; there, tutors nurture them academically before daily training sessions begin. Across these various forums, tutors and coaches try to develop and instill principles in their prospects.

Part of the Ajax model is to teach the philosophy of the club; players are taught to respect each other and to play according to the philosophy of Total Football. Total Football is the concept in which players interchange positions, keep an intense passing rhythm, and have a possession-based attacking style. Additionally, athletes are taught to protect their bodies, since their body will potentially be their main source of future income. Kids monitor their own fitness and try to avoid injury whenever possible, knowing they need to stay fit in order to remain in the academy.[27]

The mentality of the Ajax Academy varies significantly from other academies around the world. The club pays expenses themselves rather than allowing this to be a problem for the family; parents pay only twelve euros weekly to keep their children in the academy. This philosophy departs completely from the American model; the club helps support players, allowing players from poorer backgrounds to get a chance in the spotlight. Additionally, the club offers educational support, which helps to give the parents comfort, knowing their son will always have an educational safety net. Ajax supports its players both inside and outside the game of football.

The Ajax model is filled with unique attributes. Not only do they avoid burdening parents financially, but their philosophy tends to mold players into professionals. The products of the Ajax academy are humble, professional, and responsible, whether they play professionally or not.[28] Ajax seems to truly separate itself from competing academies; however, it also struggles with early bloomers despite an esteemed reputation.

---

27   Ezez. 2017. "A.F.C. Ajax's Youth Development Philosophy with Arnold Mühren - generation adidas international". *generation adidas international*

28   Ilib

Ajax has also produced players like Freddy Adu, who shined at a young age but struggle later in their career.

Ryan Babel, a former Ajax prodigy, seemed destined for greatness in his early career. After working his way through different youth teams, he debuted for the senior Ajax team at the age of seventeen. After a few impressive seasons, Babel quickly moved on to bigger and brighter things at Liverpool FC.

Pressure quickly began to mount, as the Liverpool fans had high expectations for the young man. Babel struggled to meet the high expectations set for him and was soon sold by the club.[29] His career would continue to derail as he played in Germany and Turkey. Babel never reached the level expected of him; in his mind, this is due to how quickly he was thrown into the professional scene and a lack of adequate guidance.[30]

The Ajax model is incredibly successful but still has its flaws; Babel had a bright future ahead but was ultimately failed by the academy. They introduced him to the professional level too early in his career and he struggled because of it.

Babel is not alone in his post-academy struggles, however; the academy has a history of debuting players too early. Players like Babel are introduced to the senior team too early and struggle with responsibility and mounting pressures.

---

29 Ezez. 2018 "Ryan Babel Net Worth, Personal Life, Career, Awards and Biography." *Sportgraphy.*
30 O'Brien, Sean.2019 "Ryan Babel Explains Why He Failed to Fulfil His Potential at Liverpool." *TalkSPORT.*

Babel lost his speed and other attributes early because he was severely overworked during his teenage years. He struggled to find longevity, which late bloomers from Ajax are much more likely to enjoy. The academy has created numerous early bloomers, like Marco van Basten and Patrick Kluivert, who both managed to have successful careers after debuting in their teenage years. However, both struggled with career longevity and retired prematurely.

Some household names from the Ajax Academy have reached incredible heights but their time at the top was short. Kluivert, for example, burst out into the professional scene at a young age and turned the world alight; however, his time at the top would be cut short rather quickly.

Kluivert burst onto the professional scene in dramatic fashion, breaking into the senior Ajax team and the Netherlands national football team at the age of just eighteen. After impressing in Holland, he was snatched by FC Barcelona and AC Milan, two of the best clubs in Europe. After a few years at both clubs, however, his level of play quickly began to decline. At twenty-six, he moved to Newcastle United FC, among the weaker clubs in England. There he began to decline even more rapidly.[31]

Kluivert struggled for game time and goals, eventually retiring at thirty-two—incredibly early for a footballer. Even successful early bloomers from Ajax have struggled with career longevity. They are introduced into the professional level too suddenly, which hurts their development and can damage

---

31   Ezez. 2019 "Patrick Kluivert." *Sports News*

their muscles early on. Ajax's late bloomers, in contrast, often enjoy greater success and find longevity in their careers.

Legendary goalkeeper Edwin van der Sar didn't play for the Ajax first team until he was twenty-three—considerably late for many footballers. He slowly ascended the footballing ladder but did not truly write his name in the history books until his thirties. At thirty-four, van der Sar joined Manchester United FC, where he would rise to become the best goalkeeper in the world. Since he bloomed relatively late, van der Sar better understood his limits and the game as a whole. Van der Sar continued playing for Manchester United into his forties, which is incredible for any athlete.[32] Peaking later seems to benefit players in the long run, even at Ajax Academy. However, peaking later is a sort of mystery for many clubs.

Footballing academies have never perfected blooming later. Each and every academy, Ajax included, seems to be built around early bloomers; they hope players will grow into stars by starting earlier. Becoming a late bloomer is against the grain. Our academies are built around blooming early, but players who bloom later enjoy increased career longevity and performance levels. Let's investigate how to peak later and how to best approach youth sports.

---

32 Nutman, Angus. 2019"7 Footballers Who Peaked Late in Their Careers." 90min.com.

PART II

Chapter 4:
PREVENTING BURNOUT

Sports specialization is a major component that encourages athletes to become early bloomers; athletes who choose to focus on one specific sport from a young age often bloom early. Parents believe their child will excel at a sport if they focus on that sport exclusively. Some experts do believe athletes must choose to specialize from an early age in order to have a chance at being a professional player.

Research done in 1993 by K. Anders Ericsson suggested you must enter a field at an early age to become an expert in that field and dedicate your time and effort to improving your skills.[33] Ericsson's study helped form the precedent that athletes need to choose a specific sport to focus on early. Many parents believe their child must commit themselves to have even a remote chance of succeeding professionally; the rise of sports specialization in America suggests this phenomenon.

---

33 Ericsson, K. Anders, et al. 1993 "The Role of Deliberate Practice in the Acquisition of Expert Performance." *NY Times*.

A study conducted by the United States Tennis Association found seventy percent of athletes, by the age of 10.4 on average, had already chosen to specialize in one particular sport. Another study done by the American Academy of Orthopedic Surgeons showed 54.7 percent of parents wanted their child to specialize.[34] This trend has risen over the past few years. Charles A. Popkin, a researcher at Columbia University, found only 13.4 percent of children balance youth sports evenly. Specialization is widespread among youth athletes in the United States, but the practice does not have the benefits we believed it did.

Neeru Jayanthi, a sports medicine doctor at the tennis program at Emory University, discovered no benefits to sports specialization prior to puberty.[35] In fact, if sports specialization occurs before puberty, these children are more likely to struggle with burnout, injury, and psychological stress.

OVERWORKING:
When athletes specialize, they begin to encounter problems related to overuse. This obsession with finding a sport and fixating on it becomes problematic because of the amount of effort it demands.

"Playing the same sport results in repeating the same movements over and over," says Rajpal Brar, doctor of physical

---

34 Ezez. 2018. "The Growing Trend of Youth Sports". American Academy of Orthopaedic Surgeons

35 Jayanthi, Neeru, et al. 2013 "Sports Specialization in Young Athletes: Evidence-Based Recommendations." *Sports Health.*

therapy. "This constant stress on the same spots of the body means constant stress on the same muscles, ligaments, joints etc. without reprieve."[36] Because so many children choose to focus on a specific sport, they must repeat movements over and over again; this wears out their bodies and leaves them susceptible to injuries.

Jay Hertel, a sports medicine doctor at the University of Virginia, writes football does have injuries caused by overuse, and the amount of practice done by players is incredibly dangerous.[37] Hertel believes playing week-in and week-out can cause injuries, mental fatigue, and burnout. Still, most club and school teams practice multiple times and play multiple games weekly.

Since many athletes focus on blooming early and specializing in a certain sport, they choose to join elite teams. These teams and academies expect athletes to play year-round, for many hours per week. This amount of playing and practicing is seriously straining on players.

On top of that, coaches often encourage athletes to train hard and work outside of practice sessions, which can have dangerous implications. "Children who specialize in one sport early in life were found to be the first to quit their sport," states Popkin.[38]

---

36 Brar, Rajpal. 2018. "The Dangers of Early Sport Specialization - Grandstand Central". *Grandstand Central*.

37 Ezez. 2018. "Are kids specializing in sports too early? | US Youth Soccer". *USYouthSoccer*

38 Brody, Jane E. 2018 "How to Avoid Burnout in Youth Sports." *The New York Times*.

Athletes begin to feel overwhelmed by the burden on their shoulders and overwork to compensate. As a youth athlete, I saw many kids quit a sport because they played too much or were overwhelmed.

When I was in middle school, one kid who played at the same football club as I did played for the under-fourteen team. Although we were in the same grade, he played for a higher age group than us. He was very serious about the sport and wanted to play in college; he practiced for hours on end to improve. When the time came for tryouts, however, he didn't grow up. Ultimately, he'd quit the sport entirely, choosing to play rugby instead; he'd completely burned out.

His parents and coaches alike pressured him into overworking. This made football a strenuous task and ultimately caused him to quit.

Similarly, the majority of athletes overwork themselves because of pressure to win, train, and perform well. Parents and coaches are at the forefront of these pressures, which are placed especially on athletes attempting to bloom early. Often parents play a huge role in pushing their children to overwork to succeed.

For coaches and parents, building the correct support system around an athlete is essential to their success.

FINDING A WAY OUT:
For the most part, late bloomers have much less pressure placed on them to overwork. Late bloomers rarely specialize

and focus less on sports overall, which helps to relieve much of the pressure early bloomers experience. However, a solution exists even for early bloomers.

Awareness about overworking is among the main components of becoming a successful athlete. By recognizing overworking as a problem, you are more inclined to avoid overworking, which—as I touched on earlier—can cause many problems like injuries and burnout.

As athletes practice the same repetitive motions, their joints, ligaments, and muscles begin to wear down and become more susceptible to injuries. This wear can cause sprains and muscular tears. During my time in organized sports, I faced my own share of overuse injuries.

At twelve, when I started playing football year-round, I was picking up injuries left, right, and center. I sprained my ankle and suffered many other minor injuries during that time. I was playing too much, and my ankle began to feel the wear and tear.

In a short-sided scrimmage, I was defending against an opposition forward. He had pulled off a lot of trickery throughout the game, fooling anyone who came his way. As he approached me, I angled my body and forced him out wide; I stayed with him and tried to jockey him out of play.[39] He quickly pushed the ball to his right-hand side, hoping to catch me off guard. He smashed the ball toward the goal

---

39 Jockey: verb that refers to forcing out of play. Often defenders put their bodies in the way, to force the opposition away from goal.

and I stuck my foot out to narrow the shot's angle, trying to block him. The ball flew from his boot, ricocheted off of my ankle, and I heard a snap. My worn-down ankle couldn't endure his shot. I knew I was injured but continued to play for the whole session.

I carried on for the rest of the match, trying to forget the pain. That night, I pulled down my sock and saw my ankle, black and inflamed. The pain was constant, throbbing, and didn't seem to get much better overnight. I was fitted for a boot the next day and couldn't play for another six weeks. The injury was tough for me but hardly my last. Over time, I began to understand the importance of sports diversification—playing too much football wasn't good for me.

As I grew older, I slowed down and played less overall, but I was still able to improve my game. I learned, firsthand, that playing too much of one sport can have a lot of consequences.

Additionally, working out excessively or failing to hydrate can lead to muscular damage or tears as well. Though incredibly rare, these practices can cause rhabdomyolysis, a condition where muscle fibers die off. The death of these fibers can then cause imbalances throughout the body, limiting heart, kidney, and liver function.[40]

Athletes, especially early bloomers, are occasionally thrown into intense training sessions before their bodies are ready. They struggle to cope with intense workouts and often hurt

---

40   Lee, Bruce. 2018. "Rhabdomyolysis: What Can Happen When You Work Out Too Much". Forbes.com.

themselves in the process. By understanding your own physical limits, you can gradually increase the intensity level of your workout. Doing so gradually helps to reduce your chance of injury.

Generally, late bloomers often struggle less with working up intensity levels. Unlike early bloomers, they have more time to adapt to intense training and are aware of such injuries. Since early bloomers are often rushed through their academies, they have less time to adapt to different training regimes and struggle. Late bloomers are slowly introduced to more intense levels of play, which can limit injuries and help them adapt to the professional scene. Nevertheless, early bloomers can still find such success—if they play their cards right.

THE SOLUTION: DIVERSIFICATION
Growing up, I used to play three sports, one for each season: baseball, football, and basketball. As I grew older, however, I narrowed my focus to one sport, football. Many of my friends, conversely, continued to play multiple sports. After I chose to focus on football, I began to pick up more injuries than I had before. My multi-sport friends, in contrast, remained relatively injury-free. This reality baffled me to the point of doing some research on the issue.

After scouring the Internet, I found athletes who diversify in sports have a better time dealing with injuries; some even have better performances in the long run. Many professional athletes played multiple sports before choosing one to play professionally. Tim Howard, one of the greatest American goalkeepers, never nailed down his position until his teenage years.

In Howard's memoir, *The Keeper*, he explains how he used to play a variety of positions on the football field; he played as a midfielder and forward, and on rare occasions even as a goalie. Even small amounts of diversification within the sport of football was enough for Howard, as it allowed him to use other muscles and avoid injury. Soon, however, Howard began to make his name as a goalkeeper. He began his career with goalkeeping coach Tim Mulqueen, who coached at Rutgers University at the time. Howard continued to play both as goalkeeper in travel football and as a midfielder on his school team. Later, Howard was selected by the Olympic Development Program (ODP) to begin his journey with the youth national team.

At the same time, Howard continued playing varsity basketball for his high school. He would later break into the professional scene as a goalkeeper, playing for the United States men's national team, Manchester United FC, and Everton FC. [41] Howard became one of the most successful American football players of his generation despite playing multiple sports and positions in his early career. Sports diversification is a pivotal facet of becoming a late bloomer.

Like Howard, many successful athletes play a variety of sports in their youth before nailing down one. Often, these athletes are late bloomers. Howard, for example, didn't break into the national team until he was twenty-two years old;

---

41   Howard, Tim & Benjamin, Ali. 2014. *The Keeper*. New York City: Harper.

he did not play in Europe until he was twenty-four. Since he diversified and played multiple sports, however—as well as multiple positions within football—he was able to find success as a late bloomer.

Matt Bowers, professor of sports management at the University of Texas, says playing a variety of positions or sports helps young athletes to develop. Mulqueen, Howard's goalkeeping coach, agrees: "If the kids play football the whole time, they can obviously suffer from burnout," he says. "For me, the correlation between playing soccer and basketball, baseball or lacrosse—to me that makes a whole lot of sense. Besides there being skills that translate over to soccer... it keeps them fresh mentally. It keeps their body fresh. It's a win-win for me."[42] Some coaches see the benefits of diversification from both a technical and a mental standpoint. By playing multiple sports, athletes hone different aspects of their game and gain tactical advantages. Diversification also benefits athletes physically; kinesiologists have pieced together the biology behind this phenomenon.

For developing children, kinesiologists recommend they sample other sports rather than specify in a specific sport. Sampling sports allows the athlete to take part in both aerobic and anaerobic activities, benefitting the body in health and durability along the way. As athletes play different sports, their bodies will use different muscles; this safeguards against injuries from overuse. Sampling also benefits an athlete psychologically.

---

42 Woitalla, Mike. 2009 "Youth Beat: Field Play Makes Better Keepers." *Soccer America*.

Bowers claims sampling helps players to better develop both physically and psychologically. Players who sample are less prone to dropping out of their main sport and have a stronger understanding of the game. Playing multiple sports, Bowers noted, can even help an athlete reach higher performance levels.[43]

Sam Snow, director of US Youth Soccer, notes those who play multiple sports up to age thirteen better understand the tactical side of football. The main problem is helping parents and athletes to understand the benefits of sampling sports. Since sports specialization yields short-term results, many young athletes and their parents prefer instant successes. Currently, athletes tend to focus on specialization rather than diversification.

However, many athletes who do sample have found longevity and better overall performances. Phil Neville, a former defender for Manchester United FC and Everton FC, found incredible success as a diversified athlete. As a child, Neville played football and cricket; he excelled in both sports, perhaps even a little more at cricket. As a young footballer, Neville was a prodigy at the Manchester United FC Youth Academy, among the most esteemed academies in the world. Eventually, Neville was forced to choose which sport to play.

Neville eventually chose football, becoming a member of the famed class of '92, winning a treble in 1999, and establishing himself as a Manchester United legend. After his athletic

---

43   Ezez. 2018. "Are kids specializing in sports too early? | US Youth Soccer". *USYouthSoccer*

career, Neville returned as a football manager, leading the English national team to a fourth-place finish in the 2019 Women's World Cup. As a diversified athlete, Neville learned more about football from playing both sports.

The current trend among young athletes seems to be geared toward specialization, yet diversification may soon increase in popularity; the many benefits of diversifying are beginning to turn heads.

Chapter 5:
PROFESSIONALISM AND MATURITY

EARLY BLOOMERS AND PROFESSIONALISM: THE PROBLEMS

A key part of being a professional is maturing. Early bloomers tend to struggle with maintaining professional because maturing under the stresses of a professional league is extremely daunting. Players like Anderson Luís de Abreu Oliveira, often known as Anderson, and Antonio Cassano struggled with this; they often found themselves distracted from their professional duties. A lack of professional seriously limits the potential of an athlete.

Anderson struggled with the professional aspect of the game; this damaged his growth as a player and, despite enormous amounts of talent, he never lived up to his potential. Anderson began his career in Brazil, impressing in the first division of Brazilian football. His talent caught the attention of FC Porto, a Portuguese club looking to improve their squad. He joined FC Porto but soon caught the eye of Manchester United FC, which paid a record-breaking 26.2 million dollars to bring him to England. Anderson began his career at Manchester United with stellar performances against top teams; then problems started to arise.[44]

Anderson began to struggle with injuries and was losing focus on his career, distracted by partying and other interests.[45] Media sources published photos of Anderson partying late at night, sometimes being dragged away from parties unconscious. His off-field antics started to damage his career as a footballer. In 2010, Anderson was directly involved in a dangerous car accident; he crashed into a wall and was dragged out of the vehicle unconscious. As time went on, Anderson continued picking up injuries, gaining weight, and partying late into the night.

Anderson's time at Manchester United FC quickly ended following the departure of Sir Alex Ferguson from the club. Anderson failed to make an impression under his new managers and was soon sold. Anderson's career quickly would decline, playing in Italy and Brazil before settling down with a second-division Turkish team. He had the ability to become a world-class footballer, but his lack of maturity and professionalism prevented him from doing so. Rather than focus on improving his game, Anderson was distracted by outside interests.

However, early bloomers can still find success if they focus on improving their maturity and professionalism. For starters,

---

44 McDonnell, David. 2012 "Now or Never: Injury-Plagued Anderson Ready to Justify Man United's £25m Investment." *The Mirror*.

45 Howard-Cofield, Stuart. 2017 "What Has Gone Wrong for Anderson at Manchester United?" *Bleacher Report*.

they can begin to focus their attention on their growth as a player. They must create a plan that keeps them accountable for their own growth; this allows them to focus on specific areas and craft their own pathways to success.

PROFESSIONALISM AND LATE BLOOMERS

Late bloomers are generally more mature and more professional since many of them fight uphill battles to write their success stories. These athletes often grow up in poverty, so more is at stake as they push to become professional athletes. Mohamed Salah, for instance, took a huge risk when he put his education aside to focus on football.

Salah developed slowly into a world-class footballer, and his parents began to worry about him. His journey to the top was strenuous, and as a young boy growing up in Egypt, he risked his education for football.

As a teenager, Salah played for Al Mokawloon Al Arab SC; he traveled over four hours each day to go to training. In an interview for Liverpool FC, Salah explained he only attended school for two hours daily; he spent nine hours commuting to his club and back. He arrived home each day after 10 p.m. only to wake up and repeat the routine.[46]

Salah's whole childhood was devoted to football; he had to mature at a young age and focus himself. If he didn't make it as a footballer, he had little education to fall back on.

---

46 Carrol, James. 2019. "Mohamed Salah: In the beginning…". *Liverpool FC*

His career took off slowly but his ambitions and goals urged him along. After successful stints in Italy with ACF Fiorentina and AS Roma, Salah got his big break with Liverpool FC. There, everything clicked for Salah and he found his goal-scoring touch.

He established himself as the top scorer in the league that year and earned the PFA Players' Player of the Year award. Through it all, Salah has remained professional and mature.

Coming from his humble beginnings in Egypt, Salah has devoted much of his time and money to improve the lives of other Egyptians. He has become a beacon of hope among Egyptians and his professionalism has inspired the next generation of Egyptian footballers.

Many late bloomers begin to learn about professionalism themselves on their journey to the top.

Miroslav Klose, who was playing in the seventh division of German football at age twenty, is now a model of professionalism in football and a legend of the game.

Klose slowly climbed to the highest level of European football. His family fled Poland when he was just a child; he grew up in poverty and had to work as a carpenter to help his family. Klose began his journey as a footballer when he signed to play for FC Kaiserslautern from seventh-division Homburg.[47]

---

[47] Byers, Joshua. 2016. "The Remarkably Unremarkable Story of Miroslav Klose." *The Versed*.

At age twenty-three, Klose was selected for the German national team despite never playing for Germany at the youth level. At his first World Cup, Klose dazzled; he scored a hat-trick and ended the tournament with five goals overall. Klose currently holds the men's record for the most goals in the FIFA World Cup with sixteen. However, he is well-reputed on and off the pitch.

Klose is recognized as a true professional on and off the field; he prides himself on being a role model for other viewers and other rising stars. In a match against SSC Napoli, Klose scored a goal using his hand; immediately, he spoke to the referee to have the goal overturned. After the call was overturned, Klose received a round of applause from the whole stadium. He later commented, "There are many youngsters who watch football on TV and we are role models for them."

At thirty-eight, Klose still coaches youth players and teaches them about professionalism and sportsmanship. Klose had to work his way up the footballing ladder, rising from a simple carpenter to a legend of the game. Along the way, he learned a lot about professionalism and maturity. Klose remained professional throughout his career and ended it with an enduring legacy as a professional and player alike. For players like Klose, professionalism is a key component to becoming a successful athlete.

Klose was driven and focused from the start. He also was professional from the start, and as he began to mature, he used his professionalism to be a role model for others and extend his career. Professionalism was a defining attribute of Klose's playing style and helped him build a legacy. Most late bloomers model similar levels of professionalism and maturity.

A dogged mentality and strong professionalism are essential for athletes who bloom later. Late bloomers have to focus on learning from the best and must learn to lead others by example. They achieve their goals by staying focused and working to improve their skills. Late bloomers learn from those around them; eventually, they teach others around them, too.

THE MENTAL DIFFICULTIES OF BEING AN ATHLETE

One of the crucial aspects of becoming a successful athlete lies in the psychological—rather than the physical—aspect of the game. Athletes need to have the right mentality in order to make it professionally; the right mentality helps extend your playing career and increase peak performance levels.

Early bloomers tend to struggle with the psychological side of sports. Many of them are not prepared to become senior professionals so early in their lives. Many athletes struggle in this respect, but early bloomers are especially challenged; Freddy Adu, for example, experienced his fair share of mental struggles.

Even before he entered the professional scene, Adu was forced to cope with the hostile environment around him. Backlash came with his early success. As he shined on the youth level, he was abused by many around him. Nicholas Scriven, one of Adu's childhood teammates, remembers him crying after a game. Many accused Adu of faking his age. "People asked to see his birth certificate, they wanted to take away our medals," claimed Scrivens.[48]

Dealing with abuse from such a young age damaged Adu's mentality. Bullying can be incredibly dangerous for an adolescent; it can cause severe depression, self-esteem issues, and lead to substance abuse or even violence. People aimed to pull Adu down and stop him from achieving, and this became problematic for the young teenager.

As Adu continued making waves professionally, the abuse continued. He signed his first professional contract at age fourteen, and issues with self-esteem and maturity complicated matters for Adu. As the player grew in popularity, his issues with self-esteem grew, too.

Adu received a lot of media attention in the beginning: he was constantly interviewed, written about, and received many sponsorship deals. He featured in many advertisements, even starring alongside Pelé in a commercial for Sierra Mist. As stadiums filled up, the pressure only mounted for Adu; he was receiving intense criticism from fans and expected to have an enormous media presence.

Scrivens commented, "You saw his personality change." Adu struggled with his mental health while adjusting to professional life. Trevor Moawad, who worked with Adu, said, "They had a media plan, [but] they no other plans... If there

---

[48] Helms, Andrew. 2016 "Throwback Thursday: 14-Year-Old Freddy Adu and the Age Truthers." *Vice*

was a plan to develop Freddy, I never heard anything about it."[49] Adu's career was built around media attention rather than the sport of football. Rather than focus on football itself, he had to juggle interviews, sponsorships, and paparazzi—all in his early teens.

In Adu's case, the environment was simply too much to handle; the player is hardly alone in this respect.

**

Many athletes who mature faster than their peers encounter psychological problems. They trust in their natural gits and believe they do not need to work as hard as their peers. Dominating youth sports can heavily inflate an athlete's ego, which can be very problematic, especially when prodigies fail to meet the expectations set for them. Ravel Morrison, a young star expected to go on to greatness, is one example of this phenomenon. Sir Alex Ferguson once described Morrison as "the best kid you will ever see."

Morrison bewildered everyone in the Manchester United Academy and outshone other academy prospects like Paul Pogba and Jesse Lingard, who later became established footballers. He was quickly rushed into the first team and made his senior debut at seventeen.[50]

---

49   Helms, Andrew. 2016 "Throwback Thursday: 14-Year-Old Freddy Adu and the Age Truthers." *Vice*

50   Soccity. 2019 "Ravel Morrison - Man United's Biggest Disappointment?" *Soccity*.

At the youth level, Morrison made things look easy; Manchester United legend Gary Neville claimed, "Ravel Morrison's ability was just a scandal." The teen was ranked very highly among those at the club and all believed he was destined for greatness. However, problems arose for Morrison when he was called up to the senior team.

Morrison had a falling out with the club's manager; many blamed his attitude for the problem. "Sadly there are examples of players who have similar backgrounds to Giggs or Cristiano Ronaldo who, despite enormous natural talent, just aren't emotionally or mentally strong enough," Ferguson said. [51] Despite being hailed by many as one of the most talented prospects in football, Morrison was never mentally strong enough. He was distracted, didn't train enough, and ultimately failed to meet the expectations placed upon him.

Within a few years, Morrison's career would disintegrate. He struggled to remain at the highest level of football and his talent went to waste. Like Morrison, many talented athletes can suffer due to an inflated ego. Outside distractions and ego problems can detract from their growth as athletes.[52]

All athletes, regardless of type, need the correct mentality to succeed. Athletes must endure a lot; having the correct mentality for endurance is pivotal.

---

[51] Soccity. 2019 "Ravel Morrison - Man United's Biggest Disappointment?" *Soccity.*

[52] Mitten, Andy. 2017 "Where on Earth Did It All Go Wrong for Ravel Morrison?" *FourFourTwo.*

THE RIGHT MENTALITY

Players must have the correct mentality to show up every day striving to do their best. This applies to all aspects of life as well as sports; the most successful people work hard and are willing to learn and improve. Let's consider the example of Cristiano Ronaldo—for many, one of the best players of all time. Ronaldo did not start his career at the top, however. Many people forget he had to work his way to the top.

Ronaldo began his career on the small island of Madeira, near Portugal, playing for a local team. By the age of eight, he tried out in Lisbon and signed a contract to join the Sporting Lisbon Academy. At seventeen, he was given a chance to play on the senior team, where he began to shine and went on to earn a spot on the Portuguese national team. He impressed in the preseason and even earned accolades from Alex Ferguson. However, Ronaldo was far from his prime.

Despite being an incredibly evasive dribbler, Ronaldo had little else going for him at the time. In his first season at Manchester United, he only scored four goals in the Premier League.[53] The following season he netted only five.

Then, out of nowhere, Ronaldo went from scoring four or five goals to scoring over thirty each season.[54] His success was a long time coming, however. Ronaldo worked hard every day to improve; he practiced extra before and after training

---

53 Ezez. 2019. "Cristiano Ronaldo | Football Stats | Juventus | Season 2003/2004 | Soccer Base". Soccerbase.com.
54 Ezez. 2018 "Cristiano Ronaldo Profile, News & Stats: Premier League." *Premier League,*

to hone his upper body, jumping ability, shooting, heading, dribbling, you name it.

Ronaldo is probably the hardest working footballer on the planet. "When the training was set for nine in the morning, I arrived at eight and he was already there," said Carlos Tevez, his former teammate. "Even if I arrived at 7:30, he was already there. I began to ask myself, 'How can I get rid of this guy?' So one day I arrived at six but he was already there! Sleepy, but he was there." [55] Ronaldo's incredible mentality was able to help him become one of the best players of all time. Many claim Ronaldo was never the most talented guy out there, but his incredible work ethic helped him fulfill his potential. He maximized the talent he possessed.[56]

Ronaldo is incredibly dedicated to success and winning. Patrice Evra, a former teammate, shared a story once about the team playing table tennis for fun. "They were playing table tennis and Rio beat him. We were all screaming and Ronaldo was so upset," Evra explained. Ronaldo then "trained for two weeks at home, came back and he beat Rio in front of everyone." Ronaldo's incredible obsession with winning drove him to succeed. His mentality is an example for all athletes—especially late bloomers.

---

[55] Westwood, James. 2018 "Tevez Reveals the One Key Difference between Ronaldo and Messi." Goal.com.

[56] Mitten, Andy. 2018 "Cristiano Ronaldo's Work Ethic Developed at Manchester United Continues to Be Rewarded with Real Madrid." *The National*.

His headstrong approach also has its downsides, however. Ronaldo is a hyper-competitive athlete and always strives to be the best at everything. For example, during the Euro 2016 Final, Ronaldo was injured early in the match. He stubbornly continued playing, and his injuries worsened to the point of being forced to come off. Ronaldo's hyper-competitive nature can be problematic, as it places many stressors on him.

However, late bloomers often have to compete in order to make it professionally; they often must fight to keep their place in academies or reach the big stage. Rickie Lambert, a former player for the English national team, had to fight to earn his status as a player.

Though never the best of forwards, Lambert worked hard to make it professionally. As a worker in a beetroot factory, Lambert raised money to travel to Macclesfield, where he hoped to be offered a contract after trying out. His hard work did pay off; he earned a contract and his career began to take off.

He immediately impressed with Macclesfield Town FC. Eventually, Lambert earned a move to Southampton and the third tier of English football. In 2012, Southampton entered the Premier League, the highest division in English football. Lambert was quick to make an impression in the league, scoring fifteen goals in his first season. His impressive performances earned him a spot on the England team. He actually traveled to the 2014 FIFA World Cup with England despite working at a factory not too long ago. [57] His determination

---

57 Harmer, Alfie Potts. 2015 "Top 15 Late Bloomers In Soccer History." *TheSportster.*

and work ethic helped him succeed as an athlete. Lambert exemplifies how having a strong mentality and ethic can be the determining factor in an athlete's success.

When an athlete has a strong, driven mentality, they are more able to unlock their potential. By building a strong support system and creating a development plan, you can craft a path to success.

Chapter 6:
PSYCHOLOGICAL HEALTH

Becoming a successful athlete requires having good mental health. Outside stressors and distractions can take away from your athletic performances. Fabio Quagliarella, an Italian forward, struggled with outside stressors during much of his professional career. He was psychologically tormented by blackmailers, and these problems began to impact his footballing career.

Quagliarella bloomed late; he began to shine in the latter stages of his career. If he did not face psychological torment, however, this might have been a different story.

From 2009-2017, Quagliarella was, unknowingly, harassed and blackmailed by one of his close associates. In that same year, he achieved his dream transfer to SSC Napoli, one of the top teams in Italy. He was excited to join the club of his childhood dreams, but problems quickly surfaced.[58]

---

58   Digby, Adam. 2019 "Fabio Quagliarella: A Scorer of Great Goals and Now a Great Goal Scorer." www.unibet.co.uk.

After Quagliarella's computer was compromised, he was referred to a computer expert by a friend. This did not solve matters, however, as Quagliarella would continue receiving anonymous messages for years; he was accused of pedophilia, drug abuse, betting on games, and even received death threats. Quagliarella struggled to cope and his performance as a footballer suffered.

Quagliarella was later transferred to Juventus FC, a local rival team. For the next few years, Quagliarella moved among Italian teams, criticized by fans of Napoli for leaving so suddenly. His career seemed to be coming to a close.

In 2017, Quagliarella's tormenter was exposed; it was the computer expert he hired who was behind the torment. As the expert was sentenced to prison and the scandal ended, his career began to improve significantly. Despite being thirty-five at the time—when many begin to ponder retirement—Quagliarella hit a career-high. He scored nineteen goals in the next campaign, finishing fourth in the league for number of goals.[59]

The next season, at thirty-six, he was the top scorer in the league with twenty-six goals—beating out Cristiano Ronaldo.[60] Once his psychological struggles were resolved, Quagliarella returned to his best; his story demonstrates the importance of mental health for athletes. For any athlete, confidence is essential to performance.

---

59 Ezez. 2019 "Top Scorers Serie A 2017-2018 - Football." *Eurosport*,
60 Reuters. 2018 "Fabio Quagliarella." *ESPN*.

Studies show confidence—even false confidence—leads to improved performance. According to Albert Bandura, a psychologist at Stanford University, "Perceived self-efficacy is defined as people's beliefs about their capabilities to produce designated levels of performances." As athletes improve their self-efficacy, they enhance their own ability to succeed.

Generally, confident individuals are more likely to approach challenges as problems to overcome, rather than obstacles to avoid. For an athlete, this can be crucial in competitive games.

The position of striker is among the most mentally challenging positions; their performance in any game is heavily influenced by self-confidence. When strikers are on-form, they have the confidence to take risks. They shoot from outrageous angles but often their shots succeed.

When strikers are out-of-form, on the other hand, they often struggle to score. They doubt their abilities and, in a split-second of doubt, a defender draws nearer, and their chance has passed.

When Quagliarella settled his blackmail problems, he began to rediscover his form. His self-confidence grew, he started scoring outlandish volleys and overhead kicks. He looked like a new player altogether.

For most athletes, especially strikers, confidence is fundamental to achieve. Confidence motivates, influences overall health, and can make the difference between a good player and a great one.

LATE BLOOMERS

For players like Jamie Vardy, a strong mentality was necessary to make it professionally. Vardy's footballing career began with rejection; he was released from Sheffield Wednesday FC at the age of sixteen.[61]

His dream of becoming a football player looked like a fantasy as he began working a blue-collar job to get by. During this time, he joined the eighth-division team Stockbridge Park FC and began to play part-time. His professional ambitions still looked bleak, but Vardy's fortunes began to change.

After three impressive years with Stockbridge, scoring sixty-six goals in three seasons, Vardy earned a move to the semi-professional FC Halifax Town. There, Vardy quit his job and focused his attention fully on football.

At Halifax, he netted twenty-nine goals in his first year, which grabbed the attention of Fleetwood Town FC, another semi-professional team. From there, he was scouted by Leicester City FC. At the time, the team competed in the second division of English football, but Vardy's skill would help bring them to the Premier League.

As a player, Vardy continued to work tirelessly, keeping Leicester City from being relegated to the EFL Championship. Then, in 2015 and 2016, everything began to click for Jamie. At twenty-nine, Vardy helped Leicester City—which struggled just to remain in the Premier League—win the league title.

---

61   Bearryman, Edward. 2017. "Jamie Vardy's incredible rags-to-riches story will have you welling up". *Dream Team FC.*

He scored an astonishing twenty-four goals, breaking the record for most consecutive goals in league history.[62]

As a late bloomer, self-confidence and drive—like that practiced by Vardy—is essential. You will need to understand the stages of being a late bloomer; understanding can help motivate you to stay headstrong.

Late bloomers often have lots to overcome before they can achieve their dreams. Many late bloomers encounter financial problems or rejection. Understanding these obstacles are common for late bloomers and can help you remain on the right track.

Additionally, athletes must also realize they may just be a late developer physically. Often, when late developers are surpassed by their peers, they begin to doubt themselves and lose self-confidence.

An article by psychologist Scott Barry Kaufman explains the science behind late-blooming. Many educators and scientists see ability as a static property, according to Kaufman, but he claims ability can change drastically as you age.[63]

Though genes do not fully determine ability, they can take years to fully come into effect. "The genes don't act all at once, but can take years to unfold," explains Dean Keith Simonton, a psychologist at the University of California at

---

62 Ezez. 2016 "From Rags to Riches: The Inspiring Story of Jamie Vardy." *Soccer Politics / The Politics of Football.*

63 Kaufman, Scott. 2008. "Confessions of a Late Bloomer". *Psychology Today.*

Davis. Many genes can be activated throughout your life, especially through stimulating environments.[64] Consider the example of an apple tree. In order for the tree to grow and produce apples, it must be provided with fertile soil and water by the environment. The genes in your body function similarly; they may only need the correct environment to be effectively stimulated.

A key attribute to late-blooming, therefore, is patience. You should understand that it may take time for your genes to develop. You must believe success is achieved through hard work and not natural ability. In fact, believing success comes from natural ability and not work can cause many psychological problems in the long run.

EARLY BLOOMERS
Early bloomers also have their own struggles with psychological problems, especially with rejection. Since they often succeed at a young age, rejection—when they finally face it—can be especially difficult to take. On the contrary, late bloomers face rejection very often, psychologically. Therefore, they must be better at recovering from rejection. However, early bloomers can still find their way back from rejection. By playing your cards right, you can help yourself overcome rejection more easily.

Consider the example of Francisco Román Alarcón Suárez, often known as Isco. He was scouted by Manchester United early in his career; scouts claimed Isco's technique and ability

---

64 Kaufman, Scott. 2008. "Confessions of a Late Bloomer". *Psychology Today*.

were good, but his head was too big for his body.⁶⁵ After Manchester United passed, Isco was snapped up by Real Madrid CF, where he would become a global star.

Isco bounced back from rejection, becoming a star on the Real Madrid team, which won three back-to-back Champions League titles. Despite blooming early, Isco overcame rejection; because of this, he successfully became a world-class footballer.

Psychologically, you must have a strong mentality to bounce back from rejection. You also must care for yourself psychologically, inside and outside of football. Make sure that psychologically you are healthy both inside and outside of the sport. A strong support system is essential to your psychological health and overall performance.

---

65 Robert. 2017 "Manchester United Didn't Sign Isco Because 'His Head Is Too Big for His Body.'" SportsJOE.ie.

Chapter 7:
PHYSICAL MATURITY AND INJURIES

AN EARLY BLOOMER PROBLEM
Physical maturity plays a huge role in organized sports. Some children naturally mature faster than their peers and may be faster, stronger, and bigger than them at first. However, as other children hit growth spurts and mature during puberty, early developers begin to struggle.

Prior to puberty, I struggled in youth sports myself. I always played with bigger, stronger, faster kids and—scrawny as I was—competing was difficult. Once I had my own growth spurt, however, I surpassed the other athletes. The big, strong children relied on their stature to give them an advantage. As the rest of us caught up to them, their lack of technique began to show; we, in contrast, were able to excel.

The delay of my own growth spurt forced me to hone my technique. As a small kid, I had to learn and adapt. I was forced to rely on skill and intelligence to bail me out of tricky situations; I was unable to push or shove my way out. After

I hit my growth spurt, I excelled, making my high school varsity team during my sophomore year. Meanwhile, many of my former teammates/early bloomers quit the sport or didn't make the team at all.

Physical maturity plays a major role in athletic development. Early bloomers mature faster physically, and hence are able to dominate youth sports. This phenomenon can become problematic for early bloomers in the long run.

Numerous studies from Indiana University demonstrate the impacts of physical maturity on an athlete. Researchers studied athletes from the 2000 Youth Olympic Games and tracked their progress twelve years later at the AAU Junior Olympic Games. They found only 23.6 percent of those surveyed had earned a medal twelve years later. Of those 23.6 percent, only 29.9 percent had earned a medal in both championships.[66]

These statistics tell a story: less than a third of athletes from the Youth Olympics also scored a medal in the Junior Olympic Games. Most of the winners at the Junior Olympic Games did not medal at the Youth Olympics. This data tells us a lot about physical maturity; early successes did not translate to later successes for most athletes.

When athletes shine at younger ages, their egos become inflated. They begin to believe they don't need the same

---

66   Cook, Bob. 2013. "Science Shows That Dominating Fourth-Grade Sports Doesn't Mean A Future Pro Career." *Forbes*.

amount of training as their peers, thus falling behind peers who are training.

Growing up, I encountered many kids who were excellent players early on. However, when the time came to practice our skills, they wouldn't put as much effort in as the rest of us. They thought they were better than everyone else.

In the coming years, their lack of practice began to show. Most of us improved, while they did not. Physical maturity can be a large factor in determining whether you succeed as an athlete. Many early bloomers struggle when others catch up to them physically. This phenomenon also occurs on the professional level.

Many people thought Bojan Krkić would become a Barcelona legend. In his eight years at La Masia, he scored over 850 goals, breaking records set by Lionel Messi. Krkić's success in the youth system earned him a spot on the first team at age seventeen.[67]

Krkić quickly showed why Barcelona coaches had rated him so highly. In the 2006 U17 European Championships, he impressed for Spain, finishing as top scorer of the tournament. He also shined at the club level. He scored twelve goals in his first season, scoring the winning goal in the quarterfinal of the Champions League for Barcelona. The following year, however, things began to turn.

---

67 Sharp, Will, et al. 2019 "What Went Wrong for Bojan, Once Dubbed the Future of Barcelona, at Football's Summit?" *These Football Times*.

Krkić was called up to the Spanish national team but requested to leave, describing himself as "physically and emotionally shattered."[68] Krkić began to struggle for FC Barcelona, racking up fewer and fewer appearances. He decided to change up the scene.

Krkić signed for AS Roma, one of the best teams in Italian football, hoping to rejuvenate his career. In Italy, Krkić struggled even more than in Spain; he struggled to cope physically and mentally with the aggressive style of Italian football. He was again sold—this time, to AFC Ajax in Amsterdam.[69]

After disappointing in Holland, Krkić left for Stoke City FC. The physical nature of English football daunted him, but he managed to remain for five years. Krkić hit many lows, being relegated to the second tier of English football and struggling for game time.

Krkić's lack of experience with the physical side of the game began to show as a professional; no longer was he the fastest or most-skilled on the pitch. Stories like this demonstrate the importance of honing all aspects of the game for early bloomers. If Krkić had worked on the physical side earlier, he would have found more success professionally. By finding balance, you are more likely to succeed and to avoid failing as an early bloomer.

---

68 Lowe, Sid. 2009 "Bojan the boy wonder is reborn as Barça's fortunes revive." *The Guardian*.
69 McCourt, Ian. 2014 "Where Did It All Go Wrong for Wonderkid Bojan Krkic? | Ian McCourt." *The Guardian*.

INJURIES

One of the main struggles the modern football player faces is an abundance of injuries. Many athletes receive limited game time because of injury, which negatively affects their career in turn. Alexandre Pato, for example, bloomed early and demonstrated an abundance of talent; however, he was plagued by injury, which ultimately prevented him from becoming a world-class player.

Pato was so prone to injury it damaged his development. He began his career in Brazil where, at age sixteen, he broke into the first team at SC Internacional. After scoring six goals in his first ten professional games, he began to attract attention globally.

Pato decided to move to AC Milan, one of the giants of European football. He didn't take long to settle in, scoring eighteen goals in his first season. The next season, Pato took up the role as his team's main striker; he shone and scored fifteen goals in the league. Pato seemed to have a bright future ahead of him, but then injury problems arose.[70]

According to sources from within AC Milan,[71] Pato had grown three inches and gained twenty pounds since he arrived at the club. The player hadn't expected the growth spurt, which changed his posture, and he struggled to cope

---

70 Doyle, Mark. 2019. "Why the wonderkid who was Alexandre Pato failed to become a superstar | Goal.com". Goal.com.

71 Rossoneri a nickname used for the AC Milan.

with the changes. Pato was suddenly much more susceptible to injury.[72]

Over the next few years, Pato would play fewer and fewer games per season. He would miss fifteen to twenty games at a time, barely ever playing consecutive matches. He suffered injury after injury and his spot on the team was placed in doubt. Eventually, Pato left Europe to explore, playing for Brazilian and Chinese teams.

Injuries limited Pato's career because he was thrown into the professional scene too early and too suddenly. He began his footballing career at the age of just sixteen, before he had even finished puberty. Pato struggled to cope with strenuous training sessions and the rapid growth of his body. He picked up consecutive injuries from overworking himself.

Athletes tend to struggle with injuries because of the rigorous nature of organized sports. Various academies and travel programs expect their athletes to train year-round, playing almost daily. The amount of time they spend in recovery, therefore, becomes problematic.

Rob Burger and Kenneth Fine from Rochester University claim football players are incredibly prone to all kinds of injuries due to overuse. Overuse in training can lead to shin splints, calf-muscle strains, and groin pulls. Athletes are also

---

[72] Camedda,Paolo & Ponciroli,Fabrizio. 2012 "Revealed: The Reasons behind Alexandre Pato's Injury Nightmare & Why the AC Milan Star Will Probably Never Get His Blistering Pace Back." Goal.com.

susceptible to contact injuries, like fractures and contusions; overtraining makes them even more susceptible.[73]

Given the intensity of youth sports, athletes are more prone to injuring themselves when training or playing. Often, early bloomers are especially susceptible to these problems. Pato, for example, began playing professionally at the age of sixteen; the rigors of professional football left him especially susceptible to injuries.

Pato ignored the messages his body was sending. Rather than take more time on the sidelines, he rushed his recovery. To avoid this issue, athletes must understand their limits. Most of the time, this does not apply to late bloomers, since their journey to the top is slower. During their gradual journey to the top, they begin to learn more about themselves and better understand their limits.

However, all athletes must be aware of the restrictions and limits of their bodies. Athletes need to understand the importance of self-care. Taking care of yourself is crucial to your career; you must understand your body and its impulses. If you need to stop during a practice or game, stop, period. Playing through injury can aggravate the damage and leave you at risk for further complications.

Early bloomers do end up playing through injury because of stakes. I played under many professional coaches when I was

---

73 Burger, Rob & Fine, Kenneth. 2019 "Orthopaedics & Physical Performance." *Soccer Injuries - Sports Medicine Program - UR Medicine, University of Rochester Medical Center - Rochester, NY,*

younger, and in one particular practice, I hurt my angle by blocking a hard shot. However, I was too concerned about the stakes of the game to stop; I continued to play despite my injury.

The following day, I found out my ankle was sprained; if I had stopped playing, my injury might not have been as severe, and I would have spent less time sitting out. According to physicians, playing through injury can worsen your injury or even leave you at risk for future problems. If I had taken myself out of the game, I could have shortened my time in recovery.

As athletes, you have to keep aware of injuries and your own health and safety. In general, late bloomers are more aware of the game and about being professionals, which helps them avoid injuries. They learn to stretch their muscles and to be more cautious when they play.

Growing up, late bloomers generally do not have to deal with high-pressure games and better preserve their bodies. Once their bodies do develop, they understand how to avoid injuries and succeed. However, late bloomers still have their own fair share of difficulties with injury.

When late bloomers begin to make their way as professionals, they are introduced into higher levels of play. In the case of Mohamed Salah, he became the star forward for Liverpool FC almost immediately after finding his goal-scoring touch. As a result, he became a target for many opposition defenders and was injured in a brutal collision during the final of the Champions League.

Although late bloomers generally encounter fewer problems than early bloomers, they still are on the receiving end of many long-term injuries; Salah's injury kept him out for a few months. In general, however, late bloomers are less susceptible to injury because of their awareness and understanding of the game.

Chapter 8:
BALANCE

Balance is essential. Establishing balance can help you reach the heights you desire; it helps you remain motivated and focused, regardless of what kind of athlete you are.

BALANCING YOUR LIFE

As you find a balance between your personal interests, your goals, and your duties, you will find further success wherever you hope to succeed. Regardless of your goals, you balance everything in life; for example, you must stay socially active while eating properly and doing house chores. Keeping a balance in your life is essential to staying healthy and succeeding.

Often, early bloomers prioritize certain aspects of their lives, which creates destructive tendencies. Steven Keteyian, professor at Oakland University's School of Health Sciences, has witnessed many early bloomers struggle with balance. "Athletes are obsessed and gullible," says Keteyian. "They will do anything they can to improve their performance and they don't know when to stop." In Keteyian's experience, many athletes have trained excessively and hurt themselves in the process; they end up being sidelined for months at a time.

From personal experience alone, I cannot even tell you how many players I knew who dedicated enormous time to the sport. For them, balance was never even in the picture.

During my time playing high school football, I interacted with many athletes who worked incredibly hard to improve; they played seven days a week and lifted weights three or four days. They devoted their time to football, but this devotion came at a cost. Many began to pick up minor and major muscular injuries throughout the season.

On the other hand, I took a more reserved approach. I trained to prepare for the season, but I would continue to do other things outside of football—schoolwork, traveling, and writing. Psychologically, this balance worked perfectly for me; in the offseason, I had time both for relaxing and for training to improve. Juggling these various interests made me feel rejuvenated for the new season. Maintaining a balanced lifestyle is key for any athlete.

Research done by Babin Dhas at Anna University shows keeping a work-life balance is essential for a person's health.[74] Dhas reviewed different studies from years past and found employees are more productive and loyal when they balance effectively.

---

74 Dhas, Babin. 2015. "A report on the importance of work-life balance". *International Journal of Applied Engineering Research* 10. Research Gate. doi:10. 21659-21665.

This phenomenon applies to sports, too. Finding balance between your ambitions and your duties outside the sport is key. Balance increases productivity when you do practice or play and bolsters your overall commitment to the sport. Many successful athletes have achieved by balancing their schedules.

Harry Kane, a notable late bloomer of his generation, does a lot outside of football; he avidly watches American football and plays video games in his spare time.

Kane balances his duties as an athlete with his life outside of the sport. By having other interests, Kane is able to keep himself rejuvenated and fresh every time he goes onto the pitch. His other interests keep him motivated and interested in the sport he plays.

As I investigated these various athletes, I began to see trends between successes and failures. Often, early bloomers struggled to balance their schedules and therefore struggled in the sport football. Late bloomers, in contrast, generally had balanced lifestyles and were able to find greater success.

To balance your schedule and find success, you need to build a support system to benefit you. You need to create a model that helps you balance your interests with your goals and ambitions.

PHYSICAL BALANCE

Physical stability is just as important for an athlete; keeping your balance helps you improve technical skills and can improve your athletic ability as well.

Staying balanced, ensuring your body is postured correctly, can make the difference between a good player and a better player. When football players kick the ball with correct posture and balance, the ball is cleanly struck—moving how the kicker needs it to move. If the player is off-balance, however, the ball can go wayward. If you ensure your body is at equilibrium, you can perform movements swiftly and successfully. Maintaining physical balance is pivotal for improving your performance.[75]

In football, most movements involving the ball require you to balance on one leg. As a technical player, you need to have good balance; it centralizes your gravity and allows you to move swiftly. Furthermore, recent research has shown the correct posture can help you run further and faster. Overall, having good balance can help you attain your sporting goals.

Despite the abundance of research about balance, most coaches still fail to grasp its importance. When coaches scout for players, they often don't take note of an athlete's balance; they tend to look at other attributes of an athlete, like build, speed, and technical ability. Balance is heavily underappreciated, though it's an essential aspect of succeeding athletically.[76] Early bloomers are often scouted for technical or physical attributes rather than for balance. Later in their careers, this

---

75 Harper, Leila. 2012 "How Balance Training Improves Athletic Performance." ACTIVE.com.

76 Ezez. 2017 "Develop Your Balance – It Is an Important Skill Often Overlooked." *Amplified Soccer Training.*

often becomes problematic—which can prevent them from finding career longevity.

Early bloomers are often rushed into the spotlight, sometimes skipping key stages in their development. Consider the example of Michael Owen, who began his professional career at seventeen. He took the world by storm and was called up to the English national team after a few impressive starts. Owen seemed destined to be the next great footballer, but after winning the Ballon d'Or in 2001, his career began to decline.

Owen picked up numerous injuries and began to grow fearful of getting injured again. "I was petrified of running into a channel, I just knew I was going to tear a muscle," Owen said.[77] Owen developed a fear of sprinting, one of the main attributes of his game. He adjusted his game to avoid being injured and sidelined, but the changes also caused problems.

Owen relied on pace and his finishing ability before being injured, before he feared to sprint. Once he was unable to use his speed, however, he was hopeless; Owen began playing for Real Madrid but was soon sold to Newcastle United FC. There, things didn't get any better for him.

After another disappointing spell, Owen was sold to Manchester United, where he again struggled for playing time. At his final club, Stoke City, Owen's career continued to decline and he hung up his boots after a few difficult seasons. The

---

77 Meda, Tomás Pavel Ibarra. 2018 "Honest Michael Owen Opens up about His Failed Career." Ronaldo.com.

problem, for Owen, was lack of balance—as a player and in terms of physical balance.

Owen's ability with the ball was far behind others at the top level. When he was at his peak, his pace hid his lack of technical ability. But when Owen slowed down his game, his poor skill was exposed. As a player, Owen's balance was poor; without his fast pace, then, he was practically useless for many top teams. If Owen improved his balance, he would have been a better passer and dribbler, thus finding further career longevity.[78]

Owen was not a balanced athlete; he focused on speed and finishing rather than improving other aspects of his game. As a player, he was one-dimensional, a striker who could sprint and score. Unlike Owen, many athletes have incorporated balance into their lifestyles. These athletes use their intelligence to improve the length of their careers. Many of these athletes are late bloomers, as their slow rise to the top offers many lessons on professionalism, balance, and well-roundedness.

Ryan Giggs is somewhat of a late bloomer; Giggs began playing professionally at seventeen but developed slowly into the player we know and love. He began his career as a flying winger, running past players and breezing through opposition defenses; his goal against Arsenal FC in 1999 embodies the playing style of young Giggs. However, his manager, Alex

---

[78] Otiko, Manny. 2017 "Michael Owen: 5 Reasons Why Former England Star's Career Stalled." *Bleacher Report*.

Ferguson, wanted him to improve on other aspects of the game—spatial awareness and passing.

Giggs took these comments from Ferguson to heart, focusing on improvement as a player. At twenty-eight, Giggs took part in a yoga exercise for a public relations campaign, and that short glimpse into yoga heavily impacted him. Giggs continued to do yoga for the rest of his career, honing his balance, core, and mental state. This practice helped him to play into his forties—something very uncommon for a professional footballer.[79]

As Giggs began to lose his quick turn of pace, he was prepared; over the last few years, he had been honing his passing abilities, spatial awareness, balance, and core. His manager began to play him as a deep-lying midfielder, where his passing ability and spatial awareness would greatly benefit him. Giggs was able to last in this area, as it required less sprinting and utilized the skills he had been honing. Yoga also helped him to stay fit, keeping his muscles stretched and mind sharp.

Giggs would retire after turning forty, as one of the most decorated players of all time. Yoga helped him maintain his balance and develop his game, so when the time came, he was ready to adapt. As seen in Giggs's path to success, balance is essential for any athlete looking to improve their game.

---

79 Herbert, Ian. 2013 "Ryan Giggs at 40: How the Manchester United Midfielder Did It." *The Independent*.

Improving your balance is key to succeeding as an athlete. Yoga is a great way to do that; exercises like the tree pose are especially effective. Additionally, you should look to any of your athletic weaknesses and addresses them; this can help extend your career and improve performance.

As an athlete, you should always look to improve—especially your weak points. The best way to do so would be to coordinate with a coach who could help you with your weakness; Cristiano Ronaldo, for example, did exactly this after realizing his own need to improve.

One day, Ronaldo walked up to one of the coaches at Manchester United and said, "I want to be the best player in the world and I want you to help me."[80] Working with that coach, Mike Clegg, catapulted Ronaldo toward greatness, though his request may have seemed bizarre at the time.

Clegg watched Ronaldo work on every aspect of becoming the best player in the world: in the gym, his diet, rest, skills, everywhere. Ronaldo used the resources of all the experts at the club to help maximize his potential: developing into a superstar.[81]

Once Ronaldo began to lose some of his blistering pace, he was able to adapt due to this training. He evolved into a dynamic center-forward, leading Real Madrid to three

---

[80] Herbert, Ian. 2013 "Ryan Giggs at 40: How the Manchester United Midfielder Did It." *The Independent*.

[81] Kelly, Ciaran. 2019. "Meet Manchester United's secret weapon who took Cristiano Ronaldo to next level". *Manchester Evening News*.

back-to-back Champions League title wins. Ronaldo's work with Clegg helped him hone his abilities and increase his time at the top.

By adding new skills to your arsenal, you can elevate your performance and increase the longevity of your career—as Ronaldo did.

Chapter 9:
FITNESS AND NUTRITION

MONITORING YOUR FITNESS

Jack Wilshere was introduced into the Arsenal first team at the age of sixteen and quickly rose to the senior men's national team. He left many scouts and journalists in awe of his composure and ability with the ball; Wilshere was earmarked as the next star of British football. Just a few years later, however, he would be severely hampered by injuries—missing nearly half of all possible games, as of 2016.[82]

Often, after recovery, Wilshere would return prematurely and hurt himself again because of it. Wilshere struggled to understand his own level of fitness; many early bloomers struggle with this same problem.

For early bloomers, each game is very important, so they seek to return as quickly as possible. However, learning to practice

---

[82] Hess, Alex. 2016 "Where Did It All Go Wrong for Jack Wilshere?" *FourFourTwo*.

caution—and understanding when it is best to return—is actually ideal for you and your team in the long run.

Often, returning from injury too early can hurt your team; if you play before you have fully recovered, you are detracting from your team's performances. Additionally, if you aggravate your injury and must be taken out, you waste your team's substitutions—which could cost them the game. By approaching recovery logically, you can help yourself recover faster and help your team.

Consider the example of Harry Kane.

Kane, a late bloomer, practices caution with his level of fitness. In 2019, Kane suffered an injury to his ankle in the quarterfinal of the Champions League. He damaged ligaments during the game and immediately came off to prevent further injury.[83]

Ligament injuries require a lot of time to rehabilitate, and by sitting out the rest of the game, Kane ensured his injury would not worsen. Kane took the time to recover from his injury and managed to come back healthy for the Champions League final.

Though Kane may have been slightly off his game, he performed quite well despite a poor performance by his team overall.[84] Kane reached peak fitness during preseason a few

---

83 Geier, David. 2019. "Champions League Injuries: Latest On Harry Kane, Roberto Firmino And More." *Forbes*.

84 Delaney, Miguel. 2019. "Why the Decision to Start Harry Kane Ultimately Proved Irrelevant." *The Independent*.

weeks later; he returned next season with a bang, scoring two goals in his opening match.

Kane's patience and awareness paid off. After taking his time to recover from a serious injury, he was able to play in the final match. He learned to take care of himself during his difficult rise to fame.

Kane was released from Arsenal Academy at age eleven for being so-called "chubby." Even after moving to Tottenham Hotspur Academy, coaches still had doubts about him.

"It was certainly touch and go when he was about fourteen whether he'd even be kept on," explained Chris Ramsey, former head of player development for Tottenham.[85] Everyone seemed to doubt Kane. If it wasn't for his potential and character on the pitch, he wouldn't be where he is today.

In his late teens, Kane struggled to get onto the first team at Tottenham Hotspurs; the coaches sent him out on loan a few times. After a few seasons on loan and playing with the reserve team, Kane was given a chance in the first team.

He quickly burst onto the scene and soon rose to prominence as one of the best strikers in England, if not the world. Along his difficult journey, Kane learned a lot about his own fitness levels. When he was young, Arsenal Academy released him for being overweight; from a young age, he had to learn to take care of himself and his diet. Kane's understanding of

---

85   Welch, Ben. 2018 "How Tom Brady Inspired Harry Kane's Rise to the Top." *FourFourTwo*.

his body helps him to remain fit, healthy, and relatively free of injury as an athlete.

Both these athletes, Wilshere and Kane, had to judge when they were ready to return to the game; they needed to understand their respective levels of fitness. In Wilshere's case, he judged poorly, and poor judgment only leads to further injuries. Kane, on the other hand, judged accurately; he returned fully recovered and ready to take on a rigorous training session.

In general, athletes need to understand their bodies; ultimately, they must decide when they will return to training. By listening to your body, you can help craft a successful pathway to recovery.

NUTRITION

Mario Götze, an early bloomer, had the eyes of the world on him when he was still a young boy. At age seventeen, Götze impressed for Borussia Dortmund and helped them win the German football championship. In the next few seasons, he would continue to shine for Dortmund and was called up to the German national team.

Matthias Sammer, retired German footballer and coach, called Götze "one of the greatest talents we have ever had." After a few injuries, however, Götze experienced a sudden weight gain and many of his teammates began to ridicule him. Despite this, Götze continued to impress for club and country. He then earned a move to FC Bayern Munich, where his form would be temperamental.

Götze would impress in certain spells of the season but disappoint in others. In the 2014 World Cup, however, Götze put his inconsistencies aside and established himself as a key figure on the German team.

Götze started for a few games throughout the tournament but etched his name in the history books during the final. After coming in as a substitute, Götze scored, breaking the deadlock and catapulting his team to glory. This one moment changed his life; expectations of him grew and began to pile up. The world came to expect big things from the young German player.

Götze struggled to maintain his form at Bayern Munich, eventually losing his spot on the team. Bayern grew frustrated and sold Götze back to Borussia Dortmund. Many believed the sale would bring back the old Götze, but this was not the case.[86]

Toward the end of his first season back at Dortmund, Götze was diagnosed with myopathy, a muscle disorder that impacts the metabolism and activity of muscle fibers. Myopathy triggers fatigue and weight gain, with which Götze had struggled throughout his career.

Ever since his formal diagnosis, Götze has struggled with form and receiving game time. Nutrition is a key aspect in any athlete's journey to success; staying healthy and taking in the correct amount of nutrients and carbohydrates is pivotal.

---

86 Oltermann, Philip. 2017 "The Story of Mario Gotze: a Rare Illness and Unfulfilled Potential." *The Irish Times*.

In Götze's case, myopathy could still leave a lasting impact on his performance even if he did have a nutritious diet; myopathy affects stamina and restricts the body's intake of carbohydrates and calories. Both these nutrients are essential to an athlete's performance.

Carbohydrates are crucial for an athlete as an energy source. Glucose molecules are broken down into adenosine triphosphate (ATP) molecules, which provide the body with energy. Due to myopathy, Götze is unable to obtain enough ATP molecules to last a game.

Additionally, myopathy has left Götze feeling fatigued due to a lack of caloric consumption. His metabolic disorder has severely limited his ability to fulfill his potential, despite obvious talent.

In recent years, more footballing clubs are bringing in nutritionists and chefs to ensure their players are getting the right amounts of nutrients. Clubs are beginning to understand the importance of proper nutrition for their players. I have found no correlation between nutritional practice and time of blooming for an athlete, but nutrition is a crucial part of any athlete's journey regardless.

PART III

Chapter 10:
GOAL SETTING

In order to bloom late in any field, you must lay out a plan for your future, starting with a goal. Your goal should be long-term; you can place short-term goals along the way to help achieve your larger goal. For the purposes of this book, we will relate this strategy to football, though this advice holds true for any field. In football, people tend to take two paths—a managerial path and a player path.

BECOMING A MANAGER

Managers tend to start in the later stages of their careers, mainly after turning thirty. Most are appointed later in their lives. This phenomenon can be explained through a study done by George Bartzokis, a neurologist at the University of California, Los Angeles. He proved that our brains increase in use of myelination as we age; this chemical opens more brain circuits as we gain more memories and life experiences.[87]

---

87   Kaufman, Scott. 2008. "Confessions of a Late Bloomer". *Psychology Today*.

As we grow older, we are able to use more advanced brain circuits and improve management and coaching skills. The majority of successful coaches and managers in football are closer to their forties or fifties than their thirties for this reason.

Johan Cruyff, Pep Guardiola, and Sir Alex Ferguson are some of the most successful managers of all time; all three began managing years after their thirtieth birthday. In fact, many managers become coaches after switching professions for a time.

José Mourinho, one of the more successful managers in the modern era, wasn't always a football manager. Mourinho had a short football career and worked as a gym teacher for part of his life. He began managing lower-league teams before coming to work for Sir Bobby Robson at FC Barcelona. Mourinho went on to coach both Real Madrid and Manchester United, winning trophies at both clubs. However, he isn't the only one with such an exotic rise to fame.[88]

Maurizio Sarri, an up-and-coming manager, has a similar story. Sarri worked as a banker for much of his career, managing amateur teams as a hobby and hoping to get a big break. Sarri decided to take a huge leap of faith, leaving his finance job to pursue his dream of managing. His risk would eventually pay off, as he would get his chance to manage SSC Napoli.[89]

---

[88] Ezez. 2018. "Brief History Of | Young Jose Mourinho - Tifo Football". *Tifo Football*

[89] Nathanson, Patrick and Kirrane, Kevin. 2018 "Maurizio Sarri: Chelsea Manager's Journey from Banker to Premier League." *BBC Sport*, BBC,

You can become a football manager at any age, since your brain will actually use more advanced circuits as you grow older. A career in management is definitely possible regardless of age; if your desire is to become a player, however, you have many more limitations with which to contend.

BECOMING AN ATHLETE

Becoming a professional football player has its limits. For starts, a window exists during which you can bloom late, but past that window going professional is virtually impossible. The average footballer peaks around the age of thirty; however, many footballers have bloomed later, some even past their thirties. Generally, the path to becoming a footballer begins in the teenage years, but many also begin in their early twenties.

STEP 1: STARTING YOUR CAREER

Generally, you want to be in your teenage years or early twenties. This way, you have a large window to grow and become a successful athlete. The best way to get started on the path to blooming late would be to get into an academy or try out with professional clubs.

If you lack the time or money to enter an academy, however, you should begin playing at an amateur level. Begin by trying out for semi-professional teams or those at a higher level to start moving up the ranks.

STEP 2: CREATE A LONG-TERM GOAL

The rest of the plan generally derives from your individual goal, whether that be to play in college or professionally. In any case, you may have to work very hard to achieve that goal. You must also remember, even if you end up sitting on the bench for your team, you may be a late bloomer and have opportunities further along the line.. Choosing a goal is the best way to begin your journey.

STEP 3: BREAK UP THAT GOAL
After selecting a goal, you should also create smaller goals to help you accomplish your larger goal. Additionally, you will have to adapt your goals to your own situation. For example, if you are a late bloomer, you will have to adapt your model compared to a regular athlete or early bloomer. You must remain very focused on your own game and on taking chances to play professionally. You will have to create short-term goals to achieve your long-term goal.

Consider the case of Jamie Vardy, who began his career playing part-time while still working a blue-collar job. Vardy slowly worked his way up and eventually established himself with the England national football team. Similarly, Vardy's compatriot, Rickie Lambert, worked in a factory to afford training to become a professional. Lambert followed a similar path, rising through the ranks of English football before breaking onto the national team.

Both players divided their long-term goal into many smaller goals, all of which helped them achieve that bigger goal. Both adapted their financial situation in order to achieve their goals, as will you.

STEP 4: LAY OUT YOUR PLAN
Laying out the steps you should take will help you achieve your goal. If you wanted to become a surgeon at age thirty, for

example, you would need to find a medical school that suits you and will admit you. You would then look for a hospital where you want to work and research the requirements for working there. From those requirements, you should begin to build your plan accordingly. If the hospital requires you to shadow surgeons for four or five years, you must work that into your plan. If paying for medical school is a problem, you must incorporate part-time work into your plan. Building your plan accordingly will give you the best chance of achieving your goal.

You need to understand what you will have to do to achieve your goal. Will you have to go to medical school? Will you need to train for extra hours? Will you need to be scouted? Once you've decided on a plan, you'll need to plot out your execution of that plan. Once a plan exists, you must begin chipping away at each smaller goal. However, what if everything doesn't go according to plan? What if something goes wrong?

The best thing to do is to adapt. If you are met with a bump in the road, you move around it and go along another path. If you plan to play in college and aren't recruited, for example, your plan must be adjusted. Perhaps you could attend other tryouts or contact coaches for advice on how you can improve. Problems always have solutions, but you must adapt and grow accordingly. Sometimes, too, people realize they have been pursuing the wrong goal; they too have to adapt and create a new plan.

A heart surgeon in the New York area told me about one of his closest friends. His friend was very intelligent, attended one of the top fifteen universities in the United States and earned a degree in economics. By age thirty, however, he decided business wasn't his passion. He wanted to go into medicine but lacked the prerequisites for medical school; he had to take a few biochemistry classes elsewhere first in order to qualify. After years of schooling, he is now an established, successful doctor.

If you construct a plan to suit your needs, you should be able to succeed. Even if your plan doesn't work at first, you can always find success—perhaps by changing your plan completely or just modifying it slightly.

Chapter 11:
MAXIMIZING DEVELOPMENT

A major component of successfully blooming late is having a strong development plan. The ideal plan maximizes the athlete's potential. This process begins at the youth level, the years leading up to puberty; during this time, an athlete should sample different sports to hone different parts of their bodies. After some time, the athlete will find a sport where they want to focus or figure out they have no interest in sports.

EARLY SPECIALIZATION/DIVERSIFICATION
Once the athlete has figured out a sport to specialize in, they should begin to focus on that single sport but remain cautious. "I definitely do have concerns about overtraining," states Jay Hertel, a professor in sports medicine at the University of Virginia. "If they were to specialize, I would still want them to have an offseason and probably do something else during that time to stay fit," says Hertel.[90] "I certainly appreciate the fact that if they have the talents and want to

---
90 Ezez. 2018. "Are kids specializing in sports too early? | US Youth Soccer". *USYouthSoccer*

pursue a sport in college, they will need to do that sport for a greater period of time than they're doing right now."

Hertel's advice may translate to playing other sports in the offseason or taking a brief break during each year. This practice--or lack of--can make an athlete less prone to injury and benefit their long-term development overall. A break helps the athlete psychologically prepare for the next season and keeps them motivated to improve.

FINDING THE RIGHT ACADEMY

Finding the right academy for an athlete is pivotal to their success. The academy you select can make or break your career. Different academies have different philosophies, styles of coaching, and age groups, so finding the correct one is crucial.

Over the last few years, a sensation known as bio-banding has grown significantly in popularity. Bio-banding proposes grouping athletes by developmental stage rather than age, helping to separate early and late bloomers—hopefully to the benefit of both groups.

Since bio-banding is relatively new, research has not yet been conducted on its effectiveness. However, some teams in the Premier League have been testing bio-banding, hoping to discover a new, effective way to foster the growth of both early and late developers.[91]

---

91 Doward, Jamie. 2015. "Bio-Banding: How Scientists Can Help Late Developers Become Sporting Superstars." *The Guardian*.

The aim of bio-banding is to give both groups more opportunities to shine, instead of cutting them from age-based teams, like what happened to Harry Kane. "It's hard to tell at that age what the player is going to turn into," Kane recalled in an interview with *The Telegraph*. "*I was small for my age. I was a late developer.*"[92] Kane was cut from his boyhood football team, but fifteen years later began to shine among the best footballers in the world. Depending on your progress as an athlete, an academy that practices bio-banding could be to your benefit.

The goal of bio-banding is to create a competitive atmosphere for all athletes, so they can improve by playing others at a similar level. However, bio-banding might also have downsides.

Psychologically, athletes may be at risk since they are not playing with friends or peers. Separation from your age group can be difficult to handle psychologically, especially for young adolescents. Athletes may feel out of their depth or not good enough. Some may feel socially isolated from their peers and suffer further psychological trauma as a result.

In general, bio-banding is incredibly controversial; it has physical benefits but can cause emotional problems. For this reason, the practice has not been fully adopted across all sports. Finding a team that best suits the athlete is pivotal; in some cases, bio-banding might not be the right fit. The athlete might be better-served playing on a local,

---

92 Ezez. 2016. "'Bio-banding will create better leaders and people'". Premierleague.com.

non-competitive team if this helps them enjoy the game. Psychologically, playing with their age group may be the most beneficial.

Ultimately, when selecting an academy or team, the plan must be built around the athlete. Figure out what kind of team works best for them, what style of coaching best suits them, and which sport they want to work toward. Athletes are likely to encounter three main types of coaching: democratic, holistic, and autocratic.

Democratic coaching refers to a coach-player relationship where the coach outlines a general framework and the athlete creates their own objectives from that framework. This style is generally more athlete-driven; the athlete begins to take control of their own training sessions. This relationship is most common in private sessions and can be beneficial for a player looking to improve certain attributes of their game.[93]

Holistic coaching is similar to the economic concept of laissez-faire. Under this system, the coach will create a positive environment; the athlete would then decide their own training sessions and determine their own agenda. This style is often used with older, mature players. For some athletes, this style is more beneficial, as they can improve certain attributes of their game which they want to improve.[94]

---

93   Ezez. 2019. "Different Styles of Coaching | KU Sport Online". Onlinesportmanagement.ku.edu.

94   Ezez. 2019. "Different Styles of Coaching | KU Sport Online". Onlinesportmanagement.ku.edu.

Autocratic coaching may sound negative given the context of autocrat, but you are probably most familiar with autocratic coaching. In this style, the coach has vision and builds training sessions around certain goals and ambitions. Many athletes can learn a great deal from an autocratic coach, since they imprint tactical visions onto players. Some athletes, however, prefer to control their own growth—so a democratic or holistic style is better suited to them.

Although it may be tedious to find the correct academy for the athlete, this is essential for their development. The wrong coach or academy can truly restrict the development of an athlete.

MOTIVATION
Motivation is a key component of success in any field. In sports, specifically, the athlete must be motivated to work hard and improve; they must have a passion for the sport and a strong incentive to perform well. The athlete must understand this concept in order to be successful.[95]

POSITIVE REINFORCEMENT
I cannot tell you how many times I have felt unmotivated to do something despite its importance. In high school, I often felt unmotivated to study for one of my Advanced Placement (AP) examinations. Often, I watched YouTube or played on my computer when I should've been studying instead. Other

---
95 Barker, Eric. 2014. "How to Motivate Yourself: 3 Steps Backed by Science". *Time*.

days, I would be incredibly motivated to hunker down and work toward my goal. Sometimes, athletes may have difficulty finding their drive—like I sometimes did—but a few motivational tips might increase their desire to grind toward their goal.

When studying for AP tests, I often struggled with procrastination. I was always so anxious about my progress and whether I would have time to review all the material. In *Temptation by Daniel Akst, he outlines how procrastination is a common mood-management technique. Akst later explains how we often believe procrastination helps our mood when it does not; in fact, procrastinating may make matters worse.*

Rather than procrastinating about anything, maintaining a positive attitude is far better when working toward your goal. Staying positive helps improve efficiency and keeps you incentivized. The statement is perhaps cliché but looking toward your areas of progress rather than your areas of failure is extremely important.

For me, the example that comes to mind is my process of writing this book. At first, writing a book may seem like a daunting task. However, thinking positively about the book and focusing on my progress—rather than the tough journey ahead—made a huge difference in my level of motivation. When I kept my eyes on the positives, all my doubts began to fade away. When I looked back over my progress, I realized the process was very doable and knew I would finish the book. Focusing on the positive side can make all the difference.

REWARD SYSTEMS

Researchers recommend keeping a reward system in place; when a reward is in place, the person is more likely to succeed because of that reward.[96] If you needed to write a fifty-page paper by tomorrow morning, for example, you probably wouldn't do it. If you were offered a large sum of money to write that paper, though, you probably would do it. This example is extreme, but the point stands: a reward system can help motivate anyone. In some cases, however, offering a reward can cause a decrease in quality.

For instance, I might rush writing that paper to finish the task and claim that large sum of money. The writing would be poor, but I would have completed the job. Reward systems do work in certain contexts, but in some cases affect the quality of the finished product.

If you wanted to be able to run a seven-minute mile consistently, for example, a reward system may encourage you to work longer hours to achieve such a feat. In athletic situations, a reward system can be very effective; the rewards do not need to be expensive. If an athlete wants to achieve a particular goal, the presence of a reward may spark their competitive side and increase their desire to work toward their goal.

---

96 Barker, Eric. 2014. "How to Motivate Yourself: 3 Steps Backed by Science". *Time*.

COMPETITION

Competition can be an incredible source of inspiration for any athlete.[97] Consider an example from the business world. When Apple came out with the first iPhone in 2007, the world was blown away. Quickly after, Android released its first HTC—another touchscreen phone. As this pattern of advancement continued, the two companies propelled each other to new heights through competition. In the world of football, Ronaldo and Messi also push each other in a similar way.

Messi and Ronaldo have pushed each other to new heights as rivals. Ronaldo even commented to this effect: "Messi makes me a better player and vice versa."[98] They push each other to reach new heights, competing for the biggest individual and team awards. Their relationship demonstrates the true benefits of competition.

Competition may seem difficult to incorporate into a plan, but the best way to do so would be to create a friendly rivalry with a teammate. For example, they could compete to see who can run a faster mile; by training together, they keep each other accountable. Both players may also feel more motivated to train separately, too. Adding new motivational strategies to a plan can be incredibly useful for any athlete.

---

97 Barker, Eric. 2014. "How to Motivate Yourself: 3 Steps Backed by Science". *Time*.

98 Simpson, Christopher. 2019. "Cristiano Ronaldo Talks Lionel Messi Rivalry: He 'Makes Me a Better Player'". *Bleacher Report*.

All of these concepts should be incorporated into the athlete's model. By figuring out which motivational tools work best, which sports to pursue, and which academies fit, you can build a perfect model. You want to ensure your goals are achievable and reflective of your passions. You want to make sure you can be successful.

Chapter 12:
BUILDING A SUPPORT SYSTEM

Strong support systems are essential in anyone's journey to success. Having a strong support system can make you more confident and serve as a pivotal key in unlocking your success. Self-efficacy refers to how someone's belief in their own ability impacts those abilities in practice. Tim Rees, a professor in sports science at Bournemouth University, says support systems are key to building up an athlete's confidence, thus improving their performance.

Rees surveyed hundreds of golfers about their support systems, stress levels, and confidence levels; he found players with stronger support systems scored better by one shot per round on average.

This study highlights the importance of support systems, both for improving actual performance and increasing an athlete's confidence. In each of the following sections section, you will discover how each type of supporter—parent, coach, and friend—can best support an athlete.

PARENTS:

Parents have a strong influence on our lives. For the most part, they help foster our growth and development as people; they help us become who we were meant to be. Depending on the circumstances, parents can have a positive or negative influence on us.

In most cases, parental guidance is a positive force in the early life of a child, whether pushing their child in the right direction or guiding them where they wish to go. A 1994 study conducted by Thomas Power and Christi Woolger shows the correct type of parental support can have a positive impact on a child's enthusiasm and enjoyment of sports[99]. Parents who impacted their children positively in this regard stressed the importance of enjoying sports rather than competition. As your athlete begins to grow older and focuses on a sport, you should gradually begin to place less emphasis on playing for fun.

As parents, you should support your child and their athletic ambitions. You may have to give them a nudge in the right direction, but your child should make the final decisions. If you stress competition excessively, you might create problems for your child or even cause them to quit their sport entirely. Giving your child the emotional support they need is critical.

Studies have shown parental support is crucial to alleviating stress, especially when children begin to play sports competitively. By attending their games and watching their

---

99   Côté, Jean. 1999. "The Influence of the Family in the Development of Talent in Sport." *The Sport Psychologist*. pp. 395–417., doi:10.1123/tsp.13.4.395.

practices, you can help give your child the extra boost. As your child approaches adolescence, your direct support will not be as effective; thus, you'll want to build a system that will benefit them.

This involves finding the right coaches and academies that will take care of your child, fostering their growth.

COACHES:
During their teenage years, children tend to neglect parental advice and support. Coaches, therefore, assume this responsibility, becoming the child's main support system. Studies have shown approximately sixty-five percent of coaches recommend a young athlete play competitively.[100] This statistic shows the importance of finding the right coach for teenage athletes; their coaches will play a large role in their development and progress, especially during puberty.

When parents select a coach, they should look to their results with other kids, their personality, and their qualities. Too often, athletes are limited by a coach who doesn't support effectively or give them adequate care. Although finding the ideal coach may take time, they can make the difference between succeeding at a sport and dropping it entirely.

Many coaches help their athletes to progress and improve because of their individual qualities. An example of this would be Mike Phelan, former assistant coach of Manchester

---

100 Baxter-Jones AD, et al. 2003. "Parental influence on sport participation in elite young athletes. - PubMed - NCBI". Ncbi.nlm.nih.gov.

United. Phelan focused his attention on coaching younger players at the club, like Harry Maguire and Andy Robertson. He helped to nurture them and improve their game.

A few years later, both Robertson and Maguire would sign lucrative contracts for professional teams—Robertson for Liverpool and Maguire for Manchester United. Both of them would succeed at their new clubs thanks to Phelan's instruction.

After joining Manchester United, Maguire explained how Phelan influenced him and motivated him to join Manchester United. "He gave me lots of tips and pointers from the top players he'd worked with in the past," Maguire said about Phelan. "He's got great experience and I had a really good relationship with him."[101] Coach Phelan helped to set Maguire's career in motion.

Phelan's ability to spot talent and introduce athletes into the professional stage helped Maguire develop into an established player. Phelan's experience and ability to nurture his players breathes success into the athletes with whom he works. His expert work highlights the importance of finding the correct coach for an athlete.

The best coaches can spot an athlete and understand their qualities even before they have peaked. Like Phelan, coaches must be able to spot potential in an athlete and get the best out of them.

---

101 Froggatt, Mark. 2019 "Studying the Impact of Phelan on Maguire." *How Man Utd Coach Phelan Gave Maguire His Premier League Chance | Manchester United*

Jesse Lingard, a graduate of Manchester United Academy, bloomed late; things did not fall into place for the player until he was twenty-five. For much of his early career, doubts surrounded Lingard. Many coaches at Manchester United doubted if he even belonged in the club.

Nearly ten years before his big break, Alex Ferguson, his former manager, spoke to Lingard about his lack of progress. At the time, Lingard was frustrated because many of his peers were receiving professional contracts, while he was not. He was close to moving to another team or quitting the sport entirely. Lingard recalls Ferguson saying, "It's going to take [sic] awhile for you, Jesse. We believe in you. But you're going to have to be patient."[102]

Lingard continued to push for his spot, even if he had to go up against larger, more physical players. "I can't even tell you how *massive that was for me and my family*," Lingard explains. *"You'd think I'd be disappointed, but when an absolute legend like Sir Alex says they believe in you, that means everything. He didn't have to meet with us, and he didn't have to say that to me."*[103] The belief instilled in Lingard by Ferguson turned a potential dropout into a footballing star.

Understanding the players—if they are a late bloomer or not—is pivotal for succeeding as a coach. Nearly a decade since that conversation, Lingard is a regular at Manchester United after impressing during the 2017-18 season. Ferguson

---

102

103 Jabbar, Nasir. 2019 "What Sir Alex Ferguson Said To A 16-Year-Old Jesse Lingard Is Pure Class." *SPORTbible.*

was able to understand Lingard's situation and knew how to get the best out of him. Coaches and other influences around an athlete can make a huge difference, one which often goes underappreciated. By understanding this and creating an effective support system, reaching the next level is even more attainable.

FRIENDS:
As friends, we are often expected to support each other in what we do. The three main ways to support friends in a positive manner are to encourage, advise, and compete. Each of these ways is a valid and effective means of positively impacting your friends.

I'm sure you could name hundreds of ways to support or encourage your friends. Although it does seem cliché, being enthusiastic and encouraging goes a long way. Whether it's sending a heartfelt message or cheering from the sidelines, emotional support goes a long way for an athlete's confidence and performance. Support is pivotal to relieve stress. This is true in all circumstances; if your friend is going through a tough time, for example, empathy can go a long way. Your support can help them find a comfortable place to talk and relieve the anxiety they might have. Giving advice and guidance can also help relieve stress and anxiety.

Informational support is key. When a friend or loved one gives you guidance in any circumstance, you feel cared about. This experience of care motivates you to work harder and gives you a sense of tranquility in knowing you are not alone. Giving your friend advice and criticism, as well as positive feedback, helps them stay focused and keep working toward success. Both of these techniques help to provide emotional support, but you can also benefit your friends through competition.

Sometimes, we see competition negatively; if you use it well, however, competition can be a supportive tool. Especially in athletic circles, competition fuels an athlete's drive. As a friend, you can embark on an athletic journey too; you can push one another to greater heights and you will be there to support each other on the journey to the finish line. Ultimately, you can support a friend in a multitude of ways. By being encouraging, supporting, and loving, you can help your friends achieve greatness.

Chapter 13:
NUTRITION

Nutrition is incredibly important for any athlete. Simple things like being overweight or eating poorly before a game can have devastating impacts on your performance and progression. Athletes must monitor their nutritional intake to truly enhance their progression as a player—daily intake as well as intake prior to matches and practices. Consuming the correct number of calories and proteins is pivotal to maximizing your performance.

OVERVIEW:

Calories are an important way we can fuel up and maintain our energy levels. According to Gazelle Nutrition, elite players burn 1100 calories on average during a game.[104] When players train, they often burn over 3000 calories.[105] Calories

---

[104] Eziz. 2018 "World Cup 2018: Nutrition for Soccer Players." *Gazelle Nutrition Lab.*

[105] Froggatt, Mark. 2019 "Studying the Impact of Phelan on Maguire." *How Man Utd Coach Phelan Gave Maguire His Premier League Chance | Manchester United*

are essential for your body's basic functions; if you do not consume enough calories, you may feel fatigued and your body may struggle with basic functions.

Generally, athletes should consume more calories on game days or training days; this is to ensure you consume enough calories to sustain your workout and avoid fatigue. Additionally, you must consume large amounts of carbohydrates and proteins to sustain your workout.[106]

Carbohydrates help maintain energy levels by providing the body with glucose, which is then broken down into adenosine triphosphate (ATP). ATP is among the body's main sources of energy—a pivotal source for any athlete. Experts at Gazelle Nutrition created a formula to help you figure out the number of carbs you should consume: five to ten grams of carbs for every kilogram of an athlete's body.[107]

By following this model of carbohydrate intake, you can help provide your body with enough energy to last through your exercise. Ensuring you have enough energy can be especially pivotal during long training sessions or intense games. Protein consumption is also very important and should be monitored meticulously.

Protein provides your body with the necessary amino acids to help the body's recovery after the fact.[108] When you cannot

---

106 Ezez. 2019 "Soccer Nutrition." *SJEB Soccer*,

107 Eziz. 2018 "World Cup 2018: Nutrition for Soccer Players." *Gazelle Nutrition Lab.*

108 Ezez 2019. "Protein." The Nutrition Source.

get enough oxygen to your muscles during exercise, lactic acids in your body begin to break down areas of muscles. This phenomenon creates the burning sensation you sometimes feel during a workout; lactic acids temporarily damage the tissue inside your muscles.

Proteins help provide the body with the amino acids needed to recover from this damage, so all athletes should consume the correct amount of protein. You are generally recommended to consume .8 grams of protein for every kilogram in your body.[109] This will ensure you have enough protein to recover ideally from exercise.

Keeping up with your required daily intake of protein, calories, and carbohydrates is pivotal to becoming a serious athlete. Not only does doing so help with bodily recovery, but it can also help you maintain performance levels and reach the heights to which you aspire. However, athletes must also adjust their nutritional intake on game and training days; their need for carbohydrates and proteins will have to change to incorporate extra ATP and amino acids that they need.

PRE-GAME NUTRITION:
You should eat a few hours before a game or training session, rather than just before playing or exercising. Athletes should focus on consuming carbohydrates and protein to help their bodies recover after the game and ensure they will have enough ATP for exercise. At the same time, athletes of all ages must adjust their diet to avoid high-fat foods before they

---
109 Ilib

play; these types of foods can cause stomach pains or even gastrointestinal problems. Before games, an athlete should eat one to four grams of carbohydrates for every kilogram in their body, as well as .25 to .4 grams of protein for every kilogram in their body.[110] As you may notice, pre-game intake is much higher than the typical daily intake.

Before games, athletes need to avoid bloating or overeating. If you eat too much before playing, during the game you may feel nauseous or need to vomit. Hydration is also very important—drink five to seven milliliters of water for every kilogram in your body for at least four hours prior. This practice will keep you hydrated before the game, ensure optimal body temperature, and keep your joints and muscles lubricated. However, you do want to practice caution with water intake as with food intake; drinking too much before a game can leave your stomach feeling bloated and make performing difficult.

MID-GAME NUTRITION:
You should continue to hydrate throughout the game to replenish the fluids in your body. However, you should be cautious about drinking too much water. Some experts recommend rinsing your mouth with water and spitting it out, rather swallowing; researchers have found spitting water activates receptors in the mouth that send reward and pleasure signals to the brain. These signals can help to improve an athlete's performance and can be all the difference, especially

---

110 Eziz. 2018 "World Cup 2018: Nutrition for Soccer Players." *Gazelle Nutrition Lab.*

at a high level. Experts recommend rinsing your mouth for five to ten seconds before spitting for maximum effect.[111] Athletes should also replenish carbohydrates during breaks within games.

During breaks, players at Manchester United eat nutritional bars from a company called Science in Sport. Practices like this help you replenish carbohydrates and maintain your energy levels for the remainder of the training session or game.[112] Additionally, sports drinks can also be pivotal during your half-time break; they can provide you with extra glucose, sucrose, and maltodextrin, all of which help improve performance in later stages of the game. By eating and drinking during your breaks, you can replenish carbohydrates and help your body's endurance. Monitoring your food consumption after the game is also pivotal; what you eat after playing or practicing can make or break recovery.

POST-GAME NUTRITION
Your post-game plan should vary depending on when you will next exert yourself. If you will play another game in less than three days, you should consume about .8 grams of carbohydrates and about .4 grams of protein per kilogram according to Gazelle Nutrition Lab.[113] If your next game is

---

111 Longman, Jeré. 2018 "That Spitting Thing at the World Cup? It's Probably 'Carb Rinsing'." *The New York Times*.
112 Ezez. 2019 "Fuelling Manchester United: Science In Sport Football." *Science In Sport*.
113 Eziz. 2018 "World Cup 2018: Nutrition for Soccer Players." *Gazelle Nutrition Lab*.

further away, however, you can eat less protein immediately. Generally, you should consume .25 to .4 grams of protein per kilogram to help muscles recover. You should also consume a regular amount of fats and carbohydrates until closer to game day; doing so helps your overall recovery.

Nutrition is pivotal in an athlete's pursuit of blooming late or becoming a successful athlete in general. By implementing these techniques early in your career, you'll build good habits that will help you further down the line. Early bloomers often enter the professional scene early and disregard the nutritional aspects of the game—which later becomes problematic. Late bloomers, on the other hand, learn about nutrition on their journey to the top. Learning gradually benefits them in the long run as they overtake early bloomers, finding better fitness, longevity, and overall performance. Many clubs are beginning to focus their attention on nutrition, however; this may bridge the gap between nutrition practices of late and early bloomers.

Chapter 14:
UNDERSTANDING LIMITS

Another key component in becoming a late bloomer is understanding your limits: physically and psychologically. Playing can have as many psychological downsides as physical ones; as I mentioned before, working at the same sport rigorously can often lead to mental burnout. In fact, many professional athletes struggle psychologically by playing the same sport.

Some athletes have released statements claiming they no longer love the sport they play—as a result of too much training or playing. This can be disastrous for an athlete, especially if it occurs at a young age. Gabriel Batistuta, one of the most famous Argentinian footballers of his time, once claimed, "I do not like football, it is just my profession." Batistuta lost his love for the game because of the amount of practicing and training he had done.[114] Outsiders may find it difficult to reconcile how Batistuta no longer loves the sport he used to cherish, but this sort of psychological burnout results from overworking.

---

114   Redaccin@MARCABuzz, et al.2017 "Seven Footballers That Don't Actually like Football." *MARCA in English.*

LIMITATIONS WITH RECOVERY

Athletes must understand their limits. While many athletes try to play through injury, thus increasing chances of further injury, athletes must understand playing through injury can be detrimental to their bodies. Consider the example of Harry Kane in the 2018-19 season; Kane came off immediately after his injury in the quarterfinals of the Champions League. This decision prevented his injury from worsening; as a result, he was able to recover in time for the final. Countless players at this level would have played through their injury, fighting to make the semi-finals. However, as a late bloomer, Kane knew to take himself off and rest before the final.[115]

When training for a sport, you must listen to signs your body gives you rather than shouts from your peers, teammates, or coaches. If you injure yourself or feel sick during a game, sit out the rest of that game; if a trainer is at hand, listen to them and be honest about the pain. Honesty is essential when speaking to any medical professional and pivotal to a speedy recovery.

Even if you are cleared to play, you should still listen to the signals your body is sending you. Playing when you are nauseous or dizzy can be awful for your health. You need to do a self-assessment and see if you are able to play; try doing some light warm-ups or test the part of your body which is injured. When I was recovering from an ankle injury, for example, I did some jogging and light touches on the ball

---

[115] Geier, David. 2019. "Champions League Injuries: Latest On Harry Kane, Roberto Firmino And More." *Forbes*.

before to ensure I was able to return to practice and to playing full games.

If you do not have a trainer accessible during your game or practice, you should sit out rather than risk further injury. If you feel better later, jog before stepping back onto the pitch to make sure you can play with problems—rather than hopping back in immediately.

Specialists at SportMedBC recommend you check yourself to ensure you can play. Before you return to play, you should:[116]

1) Test your range of motion:
    a) Swinging your arms, jogging, or walking are all good ways to test your range of motion
2) Test the amount of acute pain you have:
    a) Ideally, you should have little to none
    b) Test the area and rate your level of pain
3) Check swelling:
    a) Observe the inflamed location, see if the swelling has subsided
4) Check balance and coordination:
    a) Do a few tests, like single-leg hopping
5) For lower-body injuries:
    a) Run without limping to show your full range of motion
6) For upper-body injuries
    a) Demonstrate your ability to throw an object without pain or obstruction of movement

---

116 Ezez. 2019. "How to Decide When to Return to Play | SportMedBC". Sportmedbc.com.

From a coaching standpoint, nothing is worse than putting a player on the pitch who is not ready to play; this decision can truly hurt your team's performance and do further damage to the player.

LIMITATIONS DURING WORKOUTS

If you are planning to lift weights and you feel fatigued, you should rest briefly before returning or even call it a day. Countless people injure themselves by lifting heavy weights or exercising excessively. If you do feel tired or fatigued, you need to stop.

This strategy applies to practices, training sessions, and even games. If you feel you can no longer run, don't attempt it. In some cases, pushing yourself can be good, but you must understand your own limits. Recently, in a men's pickup game, I ate too much before playing and felt sick to my stomach. However, I was playing an important position and felt pressured to continue. Eventually, I decided to sit out for a bit, but it was too late; for the next few days, I would have stomach pains and would feel the urge to vomit. Understanding your limits is incredibly important, especially for late bloomers.

Chapter 15:
RECOVERY

Recovery is often overlooked by many young athletes, even though it is an essential component of athletic performance. Recovery refers to the aftermath of both injuries and every training; focusing on recovery will make you a better athlete and keep you on the pitch for longer. To recover effectively, you must practice monitoring your diet, conditional training, sleeping habits, and training habits.

Research has shown an athlete's body will break down from intensive exercise without sufficient recovery. Recovery allows for the repair of damaged tissues; without it, athletes are more susceptible to injuries. Overworking is a growing epidemic for athletes, since they are limiting their body's recovery time.

As a result, most professional teams have begun to hire sports science teams—nutritionists, strength coaches, and a variety of others. They are employed to ensure athletes are eating, resting, and recovering correctly. Professional teams are beginning to understand the importance of recovery and rehabilitation.

These specialists are hired to advise players and coaches; they ensure athletes participate in recovery sessions and use the correct techniques to avoid cramps and other injuries. These sessions help athletes recover their strength and fitness after a match or training and prevent further injury.

These coaches are hired to help athletes find balance between under- and over-training; they ensure athletes have enough time to recover between games or training sessions. When athletes do overwork themselves, these stressors can lead to injuries, decreased morale, and a drop in their performance.

SHORT-TERM RECOVERY
Short-term recovery, or active recovery, refers to the techniques used after an exercise. During active recovery, the athlete must work to replenish energy stores and fluids, optimizing protein synthesis and repairing damaged cells. Your post-exercise meal is crucial to your recovery.[117]

During short-term recovery, you should consume protein and carbohydrates to help rebuild the damaged muscles and also inform your body to begin the recovery process.

CARBOHYDRATES
When choosing your carbohydrates, you should avoid inflammatory foods like grains; they can cause chronic inflammation and hurt your body's recovery process. Instead, aim to consume non-inflammatory foods like white rice.

---

[117] Quinn, Elizabeth. 2018. "Enlist Supportive Friends and Family So You Can Excel in Sports." Verywell Fit.a

Carbohydrates help to replenish your energy stores and help you recover for your next session.

FATS

You should primarily aim to consume monounsaturated fats, polyunsaturated fats, and saturated fats. Each of these types of fats provides your body with unique benefits.

Monounsaturated fats help your body's cholesterol levels and play an important role in fat loss. These fats can be found in foods like almonds, walnuts, and various other foods.[118]

On the other hand, polyunsaturated fats provide your body with Omega-3 and Omega-6, both of which are important in your body's function and recovery. These can be found in foods like salmon.[119]

Lastly, you should focus on consuming saturated fats. Although saturated fats are controversial, newer research shows the benefits of eating saturated fats. Tokelau, a territory in New Zealand, is home to some of the best-conditioned athletes in the world due to a diet rich in saturated fats.

Additional research conducted by Walter Willett, a nutrition researcher at Harvard University, has found saturated fats do not cause obesity or heart disease. Saturated fats, which are found in numerous foods, contain plenty of energy to help your body recover; they also increase testosterone levels,

---

[118] Jack. 2016 "Soccer Players and Fats." *Optimal Soccer*

[119] Redaccin@MARCABuzz, et al.2017 "Seven Footballers That Don't Actually like Football." *MARCA in English*.

helping build back muscular strength. Rest is also a large part of recovery, as it gives your brain a break.

SLEEP

Sleep is another key element to recovery. Sleep helps stimulate muscle recovery and build up your energy again for the next day. Much of your body's muscular recovery occurs during sleep, so you should consume protein a few hours before sleeping to aid this process.

Inadequate sleep can cause hormonal changes in stress, muscle recovery, and mood. A 2015 study conducted at The Catholic University of Korea found sleep deprivation decreases your human growth hormone and decreases glycogen synthesis.[120] This data demonstrates the importance of having adequate sleep in an athlete's development.

COOLDOWN

Doing some cooldown exercises, like stretching out your muscles, is especially important after rough matches or training sessions. A cooldown should include a five-minute jog, five to ten minutes of stretching muscles used, dynamic stretching, and light sprinting.[121]

Stretching is pivotal to muscular recovery; it can help reduce muscular tightness, as well as relieve or even stop muscle

---

120 Kim, Tae Won; Jeong, Jong-Hyun & Hong, Seung-Chul. 2015. "The Impact of Sleep and Circadian Disturbance on Hormones and Metabolism". *International Journal of Endocrinology* 2015: 1-9. Hindawi Limited. doi:10.1155/2015/591729.

121 Ezez. 2019. "The Importance of Recovery in Soccer". *Soccer Training Info.*

aching. Stretching prevents further injuries and accelerates your recovery. A light jog is also important to calm your muscles down.

RELAXATION

In your downtime, you should relax—especially after rigorous training or an intense match. You should aim to reduce stress on your body, as well as any emotional stress; common activities include reading, watching television, and even meditating. Many people find an ice bath helps; athletes like David Beckham and Carli Lloyd use ice baths to aid recovery. Ice baths are well renowned for relieving swelling and speeding recovery prior to a training session or game.

LONG-TERM RECOVERY

Long-term recovery techniques are used in seasonal training programs. Certain teams and coaches will design training schedules that include recovery days or modified workouts. These recovery techniques are effective despite being uncommon.[122]

All in all, recovery is essential in reaching the highest level of the game. Many late bloomers learn about recovery on their journey to the top; they use their knowledge of recovery to extend their careers and keep playing consistently.

Most early bloomers do not focus on recovery and are injured or play inconsistently as a result. As sports development programs continue to change, however, more early bloomers will

---

[122] Quinn, Elizabeth. 2018. "Enlist Supportive Friends and Family So You Can Excel in Sports." Verywell Fit.a

be exposed to recovery techniques; this will benefit them and their teams overall.

Recovery is an essential component of training and should be incorporated into any athlete's routine—especially those trying to bloom late.

ACKNOWLEDGMENTS

When I set out on my journey to research, write, and publish a book, I did not understand how much love, support, and encouragement you need. Luckily, I had a host of family members, friends, and supporters throughout my journey, who helped turn my dreams into reality.

First and foremost, I want to thank my immediate supporters: my mother and father, who constantly support me through thick and thin. They both have always nurtured my creativity and answered my absurd questions. Most importantly, they helped me through the toughest times; when no light seemed to be at the end of the tunnel, they were there for me. Their constant love and support drove me to finish and publish this book.

Next, I would like to thank everyone who dedicated their time for a personal interview and who preordered my book; they all helped me along the way to publishing. Throughout the publication process, they were always supportive, encouraging, and critical. I wouldn't have been able to publish this book without them.

Lastly, from the bottom of my heart, I would like to thank Eric Koester, Brian Bies, and the rest of the support team at New Degree Press. They stood by me and helped support me through the publication process. They helped turn my pathetic, lackluster, first manuscript into a fully-published book.

Thank you to these people.

Gianna Lum, Weiyi Zhang, Hrvoje Cvija, Sandeep Kumar, Eunice Chang, David How, Natalia Casella, Thomas Cowen, Winnie Wong, Julie Parham, John Ginn, Brandon Cowen, Kwok B. Man, John Proudfoot, Evelyn Fong, James So, Shelly Vides, Francis Flaherty, Nan Santiago, Austin Ryan, Yin Man, Sarah Man, Michele Lenes, Reyna Chong, Alan Olague, Ho Yin Lo, Kwok Man, Ming Man, Loris Armstrong, John Castelluzzo, Michael Ferrera, Jillian Bathrick, Michael Hougasian, Maylon Gardner, Glenn Boyar, Matt Alteiri, Stephen Harrington, Angela Guzman, Phil Bergen, Justin Papp, Stephen Coulter, Ted Munson, Terry Angell, Don Napoleon, Deane Gavin, Alexander Geneisse, Matt Phillips, Eric Koester, Brian Bies, Milan Krystevski

REFERENCES

Ames, Casey. 2019. "Muscle Recovery Techniques for Soccer Players—Amplified Soccer Training". *Amplified Soccer Training*. https://www.amplifiedsoccerathlete.com/coachguide/muscle-recovery-techniques-for-soccer-players.

Archbold, Phil. 2018. "How Chris Pratt Went from Living in a Van to Star-Lord." *Looper.com*. https://www.looper.com/52138/chris-pratt-went-living-van-becoming-star-lord/.

Barker, Eric. 2014. "How to Motivate Yourself: 3 Steps Backed by Science". *Time*. https://time.com/2933971/how-to-motivate-yourself-3-steps-backed-by-science/.

Barnsley, Roger H.; Thompson, A.H. & Legault, Philipe. 1992. "Family Planning: Football Style. The Relative Age Effect in Football". *International Review for the Sociology of Sport 27 (1): 77-87. SAGE Publications. doi:10.1177/101269029202700105*.

Baxter-Jones AD, et al. 2003. "Parental influence on sport participation in elite young athletes. - PubMed - NCBI". Ncbi.nlm.nih.gov. https://www.ncbi.nlm.nih.gov/pubmed/12853909.

Bearryman, Edward. 2017. "Jamie Vardy's incredible rags-to-riches story will have you welling up". *Dream Team FC.* https://www.dreamteamfc.com/c/news-gossip/174075/jamie-vardys-incredible-rags-to-riches-story-will-have-you-welling-up/.

Bell, David. 2018. "Sport Specialization and Risk of Overuse Injuries: A Systematic Review With Meta-analysis. - PubMed - NCBI". *Ncbi.nlm.nih.gov.* https://www.ncbi.nlm.nih.gov/pubmed/30135085.

Brar, Rajpal. 2018. "The Dangers of Early Sport Specialization - Grandstand Central". *Grandstand Central.* https://grandstand-central.com/2018/sections/science/the-dangers-of-early-sport-specialization-in-youth-athletics/.

Brenner, Joel. 2016. "Sports Specialization and Intensive Training in Young Athletes." *Pediatrics.aappublications.org.* https://pediatrics.aappublications.org/content/pediatrics/138/3/e20162148.full.pdf.

Britton, Bianca. 2018. "The secret behind Norway's Winter Olympic success". *CNN.* https://www.cnn.com/2018/02/24/sport/norway-winter-olympic-success-intl/index.html.

Brody, Jane E. 2018"How to Avoid Burnout in Youth Sports." *The New York Times,* https://www.nytimes.com/2018/05/07/well/how-to-avoid-burnout-in-youth-sports.html.

Burger, Rob & Fine, Kenneth. 2019 "Orthopaedics & Physical Performance." *Soccer Injuries - Sports Medicine Program - UR Medicine, University of Rochester Medical Center - Rochester, NY,* https://www.urmc.rochester.edu/orthopaedics/sports-medicine/soccer-injuries.cfm.

Byers, Joshua. 2016. "The Remarkably Unremarkable Story of Miroslav Klose." *The Versed*. https://www.theversed.com/40720/miroslav-klose-germany-goalscorer/#.SkBQkw7Gyd.

Carrol, James. 2019. "Mohamed Salah: In the beginning…". *Liverpool FC*. https://www.liverpoolfc.com/news/first-team/283441-mohamed-salah-in-the-beginning.

Cook, Bob. 2013. "Science Shows That Dominating Fourth-Grade Sports Doesn't Mean A Future Pro Career." *Forbes*. https://www.forbes.com/sites/bobcook/2013/06/05/science-shows-that-dominating-fourth-grade-sports-doesnt-mean-a-future-pro-career/#657aa29b1fcd.

Cook, Bob. 2018. "What's Killing Youth Soccer in America Is Also Hurting Most Every Other Sport." *Forbes*. https://www.forbes.com/sites/bobcook/2018/07/16/whats-killing-youth-soccer-in-america-is-also-hurting-most-every-other-sport/#32f163651ea8.

Coppack, Sean & Eoghan Macguire. 2019. "Inside Ajax's $500 Million Football Factory." *CNN*. https://www.cnn.com/2019/02/13/football/ajax-youth-academy-spt-intl/index.html.

Corporation, Xap. 2019. "CFNC.org - Article". *Www1.cfnc.org*. https://www1.cfnc.org/Home/Article.aspx?articleId=TKZjBonzsuebU8XAP2BPAXEAiXAP2FPAX11wXAP3DPAXXAP3DPAX-&level=3XAP2FPAX6J7I3kztATGuYyXAP2BPAXDahIQXAP3DPAXXAP3DPAX.

Côté, Jean. 1999. "The Influence of the Family in the Development of Talent in Sport." *The Sport Psychologist. pp. 395–417., doi:10.1123/tsp.13.4.395*.

Davie, Chris. 2019. "Sir Alex Ferguson Reveals Anderson Was Thinking About Quitting Manchester United." *Goal.com*. https://www.goal.com/en/news/9/english-football/2010/08/21/2080655/sir-alex-ferguson-reveals-anderson-was-thinking-about.

Delaney, Miguel. 2019. "Why the Decision to Start Harry Kane Ultimately Proved Irrelevant." *The Independent*. https://www.independent.co.uk/sport/football/european/champions-league-final-liverpool-tottenham-madrid-harry-kane-injury-latest-a8940371.html.

Digby, Adam. 2019 "Fabio Quagliarella: A Scorer of Great Goals and Now a Great Goal Scorer." *www.unibet.co.uk*, https://www.unibet.co.uk/blog/fabio-quagliarella-a-scorer-of-great-goals-and-now-a-great-goal-scorer-1.1135646.

Doward, Jamie. 2015. "Bio-Banding: How Scientists Can Help Late Developers Become Sporting Superstars." *The Guardian*. https://www.theguardian.com/sport/2015/dec/19/biobanding-scientists-skinny-kids-sporting-superstars.

Doyle, Mark. 2018. "Adu, Lamptey & 20 Teenage Superstars Who Failed to Fulfil Their Potential." *Goal.com*. https://www.goal.com/en-us/lists/adu-lamptey-and-20-teenage-superstars-who-failed-to-fulfil-their-/ft7cqy37a96o18y4mootun7mm.

Doyle, Mark. 2019. "Why the wonderkid who was Alexandre Pato failed to become a superstar | Goal.com". *Goal.com*. https://www.goal.com/en/news/1717/editorial/2012/12/28/3631293/why-the-wonderkid-who-was-alexandre-pato-failed-to-become-a.

Dhas, Babin. 2015. "A report on the importance of work-life balance". *International Journal of Applied Engineering Research 10*.

Research Gate. doi:10. 21659-21665. https://www.researchgate.net/publication/282685585_A_report_on_the_importance_of_work-life_balance/citation/download.

Ericsson, K. Anders, et al. 1993 "The Role of Deliberate Practice in the Acquisition of Expert Performance." *NY Times.* https://graphics8.nytimes.com/images/blogs/freakonomics/pdf/DeliberatePractice(PsychologicalReview).pdf.

Ezez. 2016. "7 Charts that Show the State of Youth Sports in the US and Why it Matters - The Aspen Institute". *The Aspen Institute.* https://www.aspeninstitute.org/blog-posts/7-charts-that-show-the-state-of-youth-sports-in-the-us-and-why-it-matters/.

Ezez. 2017. "A.F.C. Ajax's Youth Development Philosophy with Arnold Mühren - generation adidas international". *Generation adidas international.* http://generationadidasinternational.com/afcajax-youth-development-philosophy-arnold-muhren.

Ezez. 2018. "Are kids specializing in sports too early? | US Youth Soccer". *Usyouthsoccer.org.* https://www.usyouthsoccer.org/are_kids_specializing_in_sports_too_early/.

Ezez. 2016. "'Bio-banding will create better leaders and people'". *Premierleague.com.* https://www.premierleague.com/news/58833.

Ezez. 2018. "Brief History Of | Young Jose Mourinho - Tifo Football". *Tifo Football.* https://www.tifofootball.com/video/brief-history-of-young-jose-mourinho/.

Ezez. 2019. "Cristiano Ronaldo | Football Stats | Juventus | Season 2003/2004 | Soccer Base". *Soccerbase.com*. https://www.soccerbase.com/players/player.sd?player_id=35979&season_id=133.

Ezez. 2018 "Cristiano Ronaldo Profile, News & Stats: Premier League." *Premier League*. https://www.premierleague.com/players/2522/Cristiano-Ronaldo/overview.

Ezez. 2019. "Different Styles of Coaching | KU Sport Online". *Onlinesportmanagement.ku.edu*. https://onlinesportmanagement.ku.edu/community/styles-of-coaching.

Ezez. 2016 "Early Specialization and the Science of Success in Sport." *Challenge Success*. http://www.challengesuccess.org/blog/early-specialization-science-success-sport/.

Ezez. 2019 "FC Barcelona - Club Profile 08/09." *Transfermarkt*. https://www.transfermarkt.com/fc-barcelona/startseite/verein/131/saison_id/2008.

Ezez. 2019 "Fuelling Manchester United: Science In Sport Football." *Science In Sport*. https://www.sisfootball.com/manchester-united.

Ezez. 2019 "Freddy Adu." *MLSsoccer.com*. https://www.mlssoccer.com/players/freddy-adu.

Ezez. 2017. "How does bullying affect health and well-being?". https://www.nichd.nih.gov/. https://www.nichd.nih.gov/health/topics/bullying/conditioninfo/health.

Ezez. 2019. "How to Decide When to Return to Play | SportMedBC". *Sportmedbc.com*. https://sportmedbc.com/article/how-decide-when-return-play.

Ezez. 2019. "The Importance of Recovery in Soccer". *Soccer Training Info*. https://soccer-training-info.com/soccer_training_recovery/.

Ezez. 2016 "From Rags to Riches: The Inspiring Story of Jamie Vardy." *Soccer Politics / The Politics of Football*. https://sites.duke.edu/wcwp/capturing-the-game/players/from-rags-to-riches-the-inspiring-story-of-jamie-vardy/.

Ezez. 2018 "Patrice Evra Recalls Amusing Story about Cristiano Ronaldo's Desperation for Table Tennis Win." *FourFourTwo*. https://www.fourfourtwo.com/features/patrice-evra-recalls-amusing-story-about-cristiano-ronaldos-desperation-table-tennis-win.

Ezez. 2019 "Patrick Kluivert." *Sports News*. https://www.sportskeeda.com/player/patrick-kluivert.

Ezez. 2019 "Peaking Too Soon." *NLP Academy*. https://www.nlpacademy.co.uk/articles/view/peaking_too_soon/.

Ezez. 2019. "Protein." *The Nutrition Source*. https://www.hsph.harvard.edu/nutritionsource/what-should-you-eat/protein/.

Ezez. 2018 "Ryan Babel Net Worth, Personal Life, Career, Awards and Biography." *Sportgraphy*. http://sportgraphy.com/ryan-babel-net-worth-personal-life-career-awards-and-biography/.

Ezez. 2019 "Soccer Nutrition." *SJEB Soccer*. https://www.sjeb.org/page/show/1225511-soccer-nutrition.

Ezez. 2018. "The Growing Trend of Youth Sports". *American Academy of Orthopaedic Surgeons.* https://aaos-annualmeeting-presskit.org/2018/research-news/sports_specialization/.

Ezez. 2019 "Top Scorers Serie A 2017-2018 - Football." *Eurosport.* https://www.eurosport.com/football/serie-a/2017-2018/standing-person.shtml.

Ezez. 2017 "Develop Your Balance – It Is an Important Skill Often Overlooked." *Amplified Soccer Training.* https://www.amplified-soccerathlete.com/coachguide/develop-your-balance-it-is-an-important-skill-often-overlooked.

Eziz. 2018 "World Cup 2018: Nutrition for Soccer Players." *Gazelle Nutrition Lab.* https://gazellenutrition.com/nutrition-for-soccer-players/.

Eziz. 2014 "What Happens If You Keep Playing Sports When You're Injured? (for Teens) - Nemours KidsHealth." *KidsHealth.* https://kidshealth.org/en/teens/play-injury.html.

Flanagan, Linda. 2018 "The Downsides of America's Hyper-Competitive Youth-Soccer Industry." *The Atlantic.* https://www.theatlantic.com/family/archive/2018/07/the-downsides-of-americas-hyper-competitive-youth-soccer-industry/565109/.

Froggatt, Mark. 2019 "Studying the Impact of Phelan on Maguire." *How Man Utd Coach Phelan Gave Maguire His Premier League Chance | Manchester United.* https://www.manutd.com/en/news/detail/man-utd-signing-harry-maguire-praises-impact-of-mike-phelan.

Geier, David. 2019. "Champions League Injuries: Latest On Harry Kane, Roberto Firmino And More." *Forbes*. https://www.forbes.com/sites/davidgeier/2019/05/23/champions-league-injuries-latest-on-the-injuries-of-harry-kane-roberto-firmino-and-more/#-64823f95607a.

Gottlieb, Jeremy. 2019. "Freddy Adu Makes 'Decision' to Return to Professional Soccer." *The Washington Post*. https://www.washingtonpost.com/news/dc-sports-bog/wp/2018/01/19/freddy-adu-makes-decision-to-return-to-professional-soccer/?noredirect=on&utm_term=.c14dcc3fb509.

Hammond, L E, et al. 2014 "The Impact of Playing in Matches While Injured on Injury Surveillance Findings in Professional Football." *Scandinavian Journal of Medicine & Science in Sports*. https://www.ncbi.nlm.nih.gov/pubmed/24118123.

Hancock, Edith. 2016 "How Cristiano Ronaldo Became the Most Successful Footballer and Highest-Paid Sports Star on Earth." *Business Insider*. https://www.businessinsider.com/photos-how-cristiano-ronaldo-became-the-greatest-footballer-on-earth-2016-12#real-madrid-bought-ronaldo-in-2009-for-80-million-since-then-he-has-become-their-most-successful-striker-on-record-scoring-more-than-350-goals-in-seven-years-12.

Harmer, Alfie Potts. 2017 "Seven Greatest Late Bloomers in Football History." *HITC*. https://www.hitc.com/en-gb/2017/08/16/seven-greatest-late-bloomers-in-football-history/.

Harmer, Alfie Potts. 2015 "Top 15 Late Bloomers In Soccer History." *The Sportster*. https://www.thesportster.com/soccer/top-15-late-bloomers-in-soccer-history/.

Harper, Leila. 2012 "How Balance Training Improves Athletic Performance." *ACTIVE.com*. https://www.active.com/fitness/articles/how-balance-training-improves-athletic-performance.

Helms, Andrew. 2016 "Throwback Thursday: 14-Year-Old Freddy Adu and the Age Truthers." *Vice*. https://www.vice.com/en_us/article/wnmqnz/throwback-thursday-14-year-old-freddy-adu-and-the-age-truthers.

Herbert, Ian. 2013 "Ryan Giggs at 40: How the Manchester United Midfielder Did It." *The Independent*. https://www.independent.co.uk/sport/football/news-and-comment/ryan-giggs-at-40-how-the-manchester-united-midfielder-did-it-8970866.html.

Hess, Alex. 2016 "Where Did It All Go Wrong for Jack Wilshere?" *FourFourTwo*. https://www.fourfourtwo.com/us/features/where-did-it-all-go-wrong-jack-wilshere.

Hobbs, Chris. 2019. "Importance of Balance and Stability to Mastery of Sport Skills | The Sport Digest". *Thesportdigest.com*. http://thesportdigest.com/archive/article/importance-balance-and-stability-mastery-sport-skills.

Howard, Tim & Benjamin, Ali. 2014. *The Keeper*. New York City: Harper.

Howard-Cofield, Stuart. 2017 "What Has Gone Wrong for Anderson at Manchester United?" *Bleacher Report*. https://bleacherreport.com/articles/1888282-what-has-gone-wrong-for-anderson-at-manchester-united.

Jabbar, Nasir. 2019 "What Sir Alex Ferguson Said To A 16-Year-Old Jesse Lingard Is Pure Class." *SPORTbible*. http://www.sportbible.com/football/news-what-sir-alex-ferguson-said-to-a-16-year-old-jesse-lingard-is-class-20190123.

Jack. 2016 "Soccer Players and Fats." *Optimal Soccer* http://optimalsoccer.com/soccer-players-fats/.

Jayanthi, Neeru, et al. 2013 "Sports Specialization in Young Athletes: Evidence-Based Recommendations." *Sports Health*. https://www.ncbi.nlm.nih.gov/pmc/articles/PMC3658407/.

Johnson, Sheri L.; Leedom, Liane J. & Muhtadie, Luma. 2012. "The dominance behavioral system and psychopathology: Evidence from self-report, observational, and biological studies.". *Psychological Bulletin 138 (4): 692-743. American Psychological Association (APA). doi:10.1037/a0027503.*

Kaufman, Scott. 2008. "Confessions of a Late Bloomer". Psychology Today. https://www.psychologytoday.com/us/articles/200811/confessions-late-bloomer.

Keidel, Phil. 2017 "Charting Where It All Went Wrong for 'New Pele' Freddy Adu." *Bleacher Report*. https://bleacherreport.com/articles/2327783-charting-where-it-all-went-wrong-for-new-pele-freddy-adu.

Kelly, Ciaran. 2019. "Meet Manchester United's secret weapon who took Cristiano Ronaldo to next level". *Manchester Evening News*. https://www.manchestereveningnews.co.uk/sport/football/football-news/man-utd-cristiano-ronaldo-clegg-15407391.

Kim, Tae Won; Jeong, Jong-Hyun & Hong, Seung-Chul. 2015. "The Impact of Sleep and Circadian Disturbance on Hormones and Metabolism". *International Journal of Endocrinology 2015: 1-9.* Hindawi Limited. doi:10.1155/2015/591729.

Kolata, Gina. 2008 "When Training Backfires: Hard Work That's Too Hard." The New York Times. https://www.nytimes.com/2008/09/04/health/nutrition/04BEST.html.

Lee, Bruce. 2018. "Rhabdomyolysis: What Can Happen When You Work Out Too Much". *Forbes.com.* https://www.forbes.com/sites/brucelee/2018/06/03/rhabdomyolysis-what-can-happen-when-you-work-out-too-much/#4cb07e49624d.

Longman, Jeré. 2018 "That Spitting Thing at the World Cup? It's Probably 'Carb Rinsing'." *The New York Times.* https://www.nytimes.com/2018/07/11/sports/world-cup/harry-kane-england.html.

Lopopolo, Anthony. 2017 "Alexandre Pato Has a Right to Complain About Injuries with AC Milan." *Bleacher Report.* https://bleacherreport.com/articles/2194007-alexandre-pato-has-a-right-to-complain-about-injuries-with-ac-milan.

Lowe, Sid. 2009 "Bojan the boy wonder is reborn as Barça's fortunes revive." *The Guardian.* https://www.theguardian.com/sport/blog/2009/mar/16/la-liga-spain-bojan-barcelona-sid-lowe

Mitten, Andy. 2018 "Cristiano Ronaldo's Work Ethic Developed at Manchester United Continues to Be Rewarded with Real Madrid." *The National.* https://www.thenational.ae/sport/football/cristiano-ronaldo-s-work-ethic-developed-at-manchester-united-continues-to-be-rewarded-with-real-madrid-1.718679.

McRae, Donald. 2014. "Johan Cruyff: 'Everyone can play football but those values are being lost. We have to bring them back.'" *The Guardian*. https://www.theguardian.com/football/2014/sep/12/johan-cruyff-louis-van-gaal-manchester-united.

Mitten, Andy. 2017 "Where on Earth Did It All Go Wrong for Ravel Morrison?" *FourFourTwo*. https://www.fourfourtwo.com/features/where-earth-did-it-all-go-wrong-ravel-morrison.

McCourt, Ian. 2014 "Where Did It All Go Wrong for Wonderkid Bojan Krkic? | Ian McCourt." *The Guardian*. https://www.theguardian.com/football/blog/2014/jun/02/bojan-krkic-barcelona-ajax-milan-roma-whatever-happened.

McDonnell, David. 2012 "Now or Never: Injury-Plagued Anderson Ready to Justify Man United's £25m Investment." *The Mirror*. https://www.mirror.co.uk/sport/football/news/manchester-uniteds-anderson-ready-to-justify-1143955.

Meda, Tomás Pavel Ibarra. 2018 "Honest Michael Owen Opens up about His Failed Career." *Ronaldo.com*. https://ronaldo.com/football-news/honest-michael-owen-opens-up-about-his-failed-career/.

Mendez-Villanueva, A. et al. 2012. "Match Play Intensity Distribution in Youth Soccer". *International Journal of Sports Medicine 34 (02): 101-110. Georg Thieme Verlag KG. doi:10.1055/s-0032-1306323*.

Moss, Tyler. 2015 "How to Conceive an Athlete." *The Cut*. https://www.thecut.com/2015/01/how-to-conceive-an-athlete.html.

Nathanson, Patrick and Kirrane, Kevin. 2018 "Maurizio Sarri: Chelsea Manager's Journey from Banker to Premier League." *BBC Sport*, BBC, https://www.bbc.com/sport/football/46473490.

Nutman, Angus. 2019"7 Footballers Who Peaked Late in Their Careers." *90min.com*. https://www.90min.com/posts/6283206-7-footballers-who-peaked-late-in-their-careers.

O'Brien, Sean.2019 "Ryan Babel Explains Why He Failed to Fulfil His Potential at Liverpool." *TalkSPORT*. https://talksport.com/football/478155/fulham-ryan-babel-potential-liverpool/.

Oltermann, Philip. 2017 "The Story of Mario Gotze: a Rare Illness and Unfulfilled Potential." *The Irish Times*. https://www.irishtimes.com/sport/soccer/international/the-story-of-mario-gotze-a-rare-illness-and-unfulfilled-potential-1.3019372.

Otiko, Manny. 2017 "Michael Owen: 5 Reasons Why Former England Star's Career Stalled." *Bleacher Report*. https://bleacherreport.com/articles/1310409-five-reasons-why-former-england-star-michael-owens-career-stalled#slide5.

Philcox, Matt. 2017 "Rags to Riches: 9 of Football's Late Bloomers." *90min.com*. https://www.90min.com/posts/5159356-rags-to-riches-9-of-football-s-late-bloomers.

Pilger, Sam. 2017. "The £50 Million Prodigy Better Than Pogba: Can Ravel Morrison Save His Career?". *Bleacher Report*. https://bleacherreport.com/articles/2694135-the-50-million-prodigy-better-than-pogba-can-ravel-morrison-save-his-career.

Planet Football. 2019 "The Nine Stages of Freddy Adu's Career: From Wonderkid to Wanderer." *Planet Football.* https://www.planetfootball.com/quick-reads/nine-stages-freddy-adus-career-wonderkid-wanderer/.

Quinn, Elizabeth. 2018. "Enlist Supportive Friends and Family So You Can Excel in Sports." *Verywell Fit.* https://www.verywellfit.com/support-athletes-for-success-3120701.

Redaccin@MARCABuzz, et al.2017 "Seven Footballers That Don't Actually like Football." *MARCA in English.* https://www.marca.com/en/football/international-football/2017/04/29/5904ab15e2704e8d088b4579.html.Redmond.

Robert. 2017 "Manchester United Didn't Sign Isco Because 'His Head Is Too Big for His Body.'" *SportsJOE.ie.* https://www.sportsjoe.ie/football/manchester-united-isco-133229.

Reuters. 2018 "Fabio Quagliarella." *ESPN.* http://www.espnfc.com/player/19667/fabio-quagliarella?season=2018.

Camedda, Paolo & Ponciroli, Fabrizio. 2012 "Revealed: The Reasons behind Alexandre Pato's Injury Nightmare & Why the AC Milan Star Will Probably Never Get His Blistering Pace Back." *Goal.com.* https://www.goal.com/en/news/1717/editorial/2012/02/14/2905206/revealed-the-reasons-behind-alexandre-patos-injury-nightmare-why-.

Schoenfeld, Bruce, 2011 "Freddy Adu." *ESPN.* http://www.espnfc.com/player/102098/freddy-adu?season=2011.

Schulder, Michael. 2017 "The Late-Bloomer Advantage in Sports." *HuffPost.* https://www.huffpost.com/entry/the-latebloomer-advantage_b_9823272?guccounter=1&guce_referrer=aHR0cHM6Ly93d-3cuZ29vZ2xlLmNvbS8&guce_referrer_sig=AQAAAEtQOO-iEz0l-HIjC3PpBALP56Ea98m2sAPaHuGUu36KpeuzFs0RdLc_tPZOkj-cEu9hs-KnSJRTbGfkwdiRixC_UWZFbzKDW_JywA8LR1HS6cF-DgK44eEHDJtpZ7PlLy4-smGyx01AvnORuIWMwgLuR35n0ck1tX_zG3p51gNctLa.

Sharp, Will, et al. 2019 "What Went Wrong for Bojan, Once Dubbed the Future of Barcelona, at Football's Summit?" *These Football Times.* https://thesefootballtimes.co/2019/08/12/what-went-wrong-for-bojan-once-dubbed-the-future-of-barcelona-at-footballs-summit/.

Simpson, Christopher. 2019. "Cristiano Ronaldo Talks Lionel Messi Rivalry: He 'Makes Me a Better Player.'" *Bleacher Report.* https://bleacherreport.com/articles/2850620-cristiano-ronaldo-talks-lionel-messi-rivalry-he-makes-me-a-better-player.

Skipjack. 2015 "The Fall and Rise of Harry Kane." *Cartilage Free Captain.* https://cartilagefreecaptain.sbnation.com/2015/3/3/8126745/tottenham-hotspur-harry-kane-rise-fall.

Sokolove, Michael. 2010 "How a Soccer Star Is Made." *The New York Times.* https://www.nytimes.com/2010/06/06/magazine/06Soccer-t.html?emc=eta1.

Trombley, Hannah. 2017. "Overtraining and Overuse Injuries Causes Burnout in a Young Athlete". Samford.edu. https://www.samford.edu/sports-analytics/fans/2017/Overtraining-and-Overuse-Injuries-Causes-Burnout-in-a-Young-Athlete.

Westwood, James. 2018 "Tevez Reveals the One Key Difference between Ronaldo and Messi." Goal.com. https://www.goal.com/en-us/news/tevez-declares-the-one-key-difference-between-ronaldo-and/n1yw3zdpiplrzjxdor4yo8th.

Firestone, Lisa. 2013 "The Dangers of Narcissistic Parents." *Psychology Today*. https://www.psychologytoday.com/us/blog/compassion-matters/201304/the-dangers-narcissistic-parents.

Alves, Daniel. 2017 "The Secret: By Dani Alves." *The Players' Tribune*. https://www.theplayerstribune.com/en-us/articles/dani-alves-juventus-the-secret.

Thompson, Derek. 2018 "American Meritocracy Is Killing Youth Sports." *The Atlantic*. https://www.theatlantic.com/ideas/archive/2018/11/income-inequality-explains-decline-youth-sports/574975/.

Togher, Liam, et al. 2019 "Freddy Adu: the Ultimate Case of Unfulfilled Potential." *Football Bloody Hell*. https://footballbh.net/2019/02/13/what-happened-to-freddy-adu/.

Soccity. 2019 "Ravel Morrison - Man United's Biggest Disappointment?" *Soccity*. https://www.soccity.net/features/2019/04/12/ravel-morrison-wasted-talent/.

Welch, Ben. 2018 "How Tom Brady Inspired Harry Kane's Rise to the Top." *FourFourTwo*. https://www.fourfourtwo.com/us/performance/training/how-tom-brady-inspired-harry-kanes-rise-top.

Woitalla, Mike. 2009 "Youth Beat: Field Play Makes Better Keepers." *Soccer America*. https://www.socceramerica.com/publications/article/30861/youth-beat-field-play-makes-better-keepers.html.

www.ingramcontent.com/pod-product-compliance
Lightning Source LLC
LaVergne TN
LVHW011832060526
838200LV00053B/3990